Learning From the Light

D1531239

Learning From the Light

Pre-Death Experiences, Prophecies, and Angelic Messages of Hope

By Dr. John Lerma

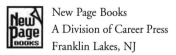
New Page Books
A Division of Career Press
Franklin Lakes, NJ

LEARNING FROM THE LIGHT
Cover design by Dutton and Sherman
Printed in the U.S.A.

To order this title, please call toll-free 1-800-CAREER-1 (NJ and Canada: 201-848-0310) to order using VISA or MasterCard, or for further information on books from Career Press.

The Career Press, Inc., 3 Tice Road, PO Box 687,
Franklin Lakes, NJ 07417
www.careerpress.com
www.newpagebooks.com

Library of Congress Cataloging-in-Publication Data

Lerma, John.
    Learning from the light : pre-death experiences, prophecies, and angelic messages of hope / by John Lerma.
        p. cm.
    ISBN 978-1-60163-069-8
        1. Near-death experiences—Anecdotes. I. Title.

BL535.L434 2009
133.901'3--dc22
                                                          2009001706

*Dedicated to the heroes in my life,
Mary and Jesus.*

Acknowledgments

To all the beautiful souls that allowed me to be part of their earthly and heavenly journeys, I would like to extend my most sincere thanks and love. The desire to share their physical, emotional, social, and spiritual experiences will always be seared into my very essence, and I will not cease in sharing the wisdom and insight they selflessly revealed. In this way, their memories will never die, and the divine messages they have imparted, I am sure, will in some way affect all souls to accept that death is not to be feared, but fully embraced with the understanding that it is the beginning of an eternal life with our all-loving, all-forgiving, and non-condemning God.

First of all, to a true loving husband and father, Dad, I miss you and love you very much. I know I will see you at my bedside when God calls me back home. Mom, you are the epitome of passion, courage, integrity, devotion, and love. Mom and Dad, from the bottom of my heart, thank you for always being there for me and for the loving sacrifices you made so I would have the opportunity to realize the things God had sketched into my heart. To my two sisters, Ana and Carmen, my brother, Dr. Hector, and my two aunts, Dorina and Diane, what can I say except that I am in awe of the unconditional love we have for each other and how blessed we truly are. Your selfless attitudes have empowered me to love and forgive without condition, without judgment, and without condemnation.

I would also like to thank the angels in my life, Mark Daniel, Ariana Gabrielle, and Daniella Alyssa, for helping me write and edit these stories, as well as for taking time before and after school to help comfort many of my patients who were dying. Their selfless desire to help another human being will never be forgotten. I am so blessed to have such loving and compassionate children, and I thank God daily for allowing me to experience true, unabated, unconditional, and sacred love. Their mother, Ana Cuellar, and the matriarch of the family, Ino Cuellar, are truly gifts from God. Their love and support will never be forgotten.

Last but not least, to all the nurses who have devoted their lives in preparing both the terminally ill and their families for their long-awaited journey back home with God and all his angels. The following are some of these earth angels: Sheryl LeBaron, Brandi Zoeller, Richard Pare, Dee Elliott, Mary Lopez, Leslie Marks, Irma Rodea, Janice Turner, and Karen Merchant.

Most importantly, thank you Jesus for my children and family, for healing me, for forgiving me, for protecting me, for holding me, for carrying me, for loving me, and for using this book to open my eyes and heart to how much you really love all of us.

*Science without religion is lame,
religion without science is blind.*

—Albert Einstein

Contents

Introduction

Do you wonder what it will be like, or more importantly, what will happen to our consciousness after our bodies take their last breaths? As we depart this world, will we finally have the answers to all of mankind's questions? Will we come to fully realize that the Kingdom of God or heaven has always existed within us, around us, but never at a distance from us? Was Mary Magdalene right when she spoke of her awakening to God's spirit being the principal element needed in creating heaven on Earth? If individual awakening is needed to fashion the presence of the heavenly realm amongst us, then is collective spiritual awakening the article of faith needed to usher in the second coming of Christ?

As in *Into the Light*, and now *Learning From the Light*, my patients continue conveying, selflessly and with great enthusiasm, a score of angelic messages that not only answer the above questions, but, more importantly, instruct us on how to create heaven on earth. Most of my patients repeatedly talked about this latter theme and how merely seeking reconciliation, self-forgiveness, and self-love, one would be able to shape their external and internal physical realm into that of the kingdom of heaven. One of my patients by the name of Katarina said it best: "This joyful and more fruitful life is what the divine power of free-will within our souls can create. All one has to do is believe and choose. As easy as it seems to live a heavenly life while on earth, many choose to not believe and at the end of the day, they desire an earthly life. When one is dying like me, the filter to the next world is lifted at which point they are privy to 'the answer key of sorts to our earthly life exam' and come to the final understanding of the Divine-driven personal and collective human purpose. If one can find self-forgiveness and self-love as on reviews their life before releasing their spirit, their transition will be painless and exalting. The opposite is also true."

Since the release of *Into the Light*, countless readers have made inquiries into whether I have continued to document the patients' angelic encounters and messages, and whether they elaborate on the two most important virtues essential for a peaceful transition, self-forgiveness and self-love. In response to these requests, I selected several angelic stories, which focused on the importance of self-forgiveness, self-love, and how learning to overcome one's self-serving ego allowed for the succession of one's divine virtues. Many of the angelic messages and life reviews emphasized the reconciliation of our two polar opposites, the ego and our divine-self. The ego was necessary for assuring our early survival as humans, and, as soon as our higher self began to develop, it assured one of an internal war of our selfish self versus our all-loving and all-forgiving higher self. It was this internal conflict or struggle that our religious leaders called our sinful egoistic nature versus our higher divine nature. As my patients stated, these two opposing sides, within every human being, were more commonly referred to as, evil versus good.

My studies confirmed that a large number of terminally ill patients who lead selfish, hateful, jealous, bitter, guilt-ridden, and vengeful lives, often struggled with finding self-forgiveness and self-love. Those patients who seemingly had a peaceful transition from this world to the next were found to have attempted to live a life filled with humility, gentleness, kindness, and a desire to do good. It was for these reasons that I elected to share these findings and messages with the world. I wanted humanity to understand how to secure a joyful and tranquil journey back home. There was no doubt that to accomplish a peaceful transition both the mechanics of the human ego and our higher awareness required the comprehension of both the proliferation of this higher self, which secured our oneness with God's spirit and all his souls, and the unyielding desire to love everything and everyone.

None of the patients featured in *Learning From the Light* are still living at the time of this writing, and most of the stories took place within the last weeks to months of their lives. Due to the unusually personal nature of these accounts, names and personal details have been changed to protect the deceased and their families. I hope you will find these stories and messages from the angels to be inspiring, encouraging, and life-transforming.

Part I

Angel Stories

1 My Father's Journey Back Home

It was the beginning of August 2007, and already the temperature in the Rio Grande Valley was exceeding the century mark. As usual, my dad made certain that his "pride and joy," the tropical foliage in our yard, was carefully manicured and protected from the scorching heat. At the end of each summer day, as the blue sky transformed into a Texas Longhorn-orange hue, my father finished his ritual by drinking a glass of red wine on the veranda while capturing the beauty of the surrounding verdure. This spiritual ceremony of sorts brought immense peace and joy to my father, as he felt the loving energy that radiated from the flora and fauna was of divine origin.

On August 10, 2007, my father would have the first of several spiritual experiences before taking his journey back home. As I remember it, my dad told me that he decided to get a reprieve from the record heat by going into the house to cool off with a tall glass of homemade lemonade and an invigorating shower. Afterward, he said he sat on his bed to read his newspaper, but within minutes he had fallen asleep. It was shortly after falling asleep that he was awakened by the sound of footsteps and voices coming from the hallway just outside his bedroom. For some reason, not once did it cross his mind that someone had broken into the house. Instead, he described feeling an incredible sense of peace and warmth emanating from the hallway. Still relatively strong for an 82-year-old man, my father jumped out of bed with a sense of jovial expectation, and, as he walked out of his bedroom, his eyes locked onto the cerulean blue eyes of what he described as a tall, well-built gentleman in his 50s, who was facing him and smiling.

My dad, always cordial, said hello and asked if he could help him. The gentleman answered, "Johnnie, this is Hannity. We were in the navy together during WWII, where I died in an airplane crash." My dad was taken aback and, with his mouth open, he reluctantly asked, "What are you doing here?"

"I need to go, but I wanted to tell you we will be back shortly to guide you back home. Do not worry, God loves you as I do." My father then saw his friend Hannity, who, with his right hand, summoned someone to join him. My father described seeing a younger gentleman wearing an Army-type uniform surface from behind him. In a swift, flowing manner, he moved clear across the living room to the kitchen along with Hannity and disappeared through one of the den's walls. The entire experience lasted six seconds, but my dad felt that it lasted for hours. My dad described a residual sense of warmth, peace, and a tingling feeling, which felt like a subtle electrical charge of sorts.

My father stood in the hallway for a few minutes attempting to regain his composure. "Son, following this experience, I felt no pain for several minutes and actually wondered if I was in my body. I felt so light and unrestricted, and my entire being was filled with an overwhelming sense of comfort and hope. The hope I was filled with spoke to me and allowed me to feel God's plan. It was truly amazing." After several minutes, my dad said he began to feel the restriction of his body, as well as pain, so he shook his head, and under his breath said, "I must be dreaming." He walked back to his bed, picked up the newspaper, and started where he had left off.

Later that week my dad's breathing worsened and he became weaker. I suggested that he visit his cardiologist as soon as possible and have him call me with the assessment. Quite concerned, my mother took him to his appointment, where he was immediately evaluated. Shortly after his exam, the cardiologist phoned me; he was concerned with my dad's heart condition. His aortic valve was now at a critical stage of stenosis, and, because of his previous heart attack, he was not a candidate for surgery. Instead, he was now a candidate for hospice care. Unsure of how my dad was taking the news, I prepared myself to comfort him as I had done with so many others throughout my years as a hospice physician. The only difference was that this time it was my father.

When my father took the phone and said hello, I closed my eyes for a brief moment and immersed myself in his cute way of saying hello. How many times had I heard it? I wasn't sure. When we began to talk, I was amazed at how he was unbothered by the news: "Son, I am not worried, so don't you or anyone else worry. You see, I have known about my heart condition for more than a year and had chosen not to tell the family, as surgery was not an option. I am sorry for keeping this from you, but I knew your mother would get sick and falter. I could not do that to her or you." Having been married more than 50 years, my dad loved my mom dearly, and never wanted to bother or worry her. A man like no other man, he was willing to suffer quietly for others he loved.

Within 24 hours, I was on my way from Houston to Brownsville, Texas. Driving home, I called my dad and had a long uninterrupted conversation with him. The following is the most profound and heart-felt advice my dad ever gave me. Because of it, I am writing it here out of his request to share it with the world.

"Dad, so you knew you were dying for the last year. Why didn't you tell me?"

"There was nothing more the doctor could do, so I chose to give it up to God and replace it with joy. I was not going to let my terminal illness steal my joy or hurt my family. Especially your mom. My joy was to be a sort of quiet calmness, that translated to peace, and it is peace that allows one to handle any situation without anxiety and with trust that God is leading my every step and thought toward his heart."

"Oh, Dad. You know I would have understood and would have joined you in your journey. That's what I do for a living. It's my calling and passion."

"Yes, Son, but you have never gone through this journey with your father. I did what I thought would be less painful for all of you, including myself. It would be too uncomfortable to know that every one of you would be depressed and begin treating me different. You know, like I was dying. I didn't want to see all of you and your mother crying and changing your lives for me. I love all of you just the way you are. I am so proud of all that your sisters and your brother and you have accomplished. I am especially so proud of your mom for being so bold, courageous, and passionate with regard to pursuing her dream of higher education, and late in her life. She is now a successful businesswoman, who is joyful about believing that God would help her be all he wanted her to be and more. Today, she is recognized for her contributions to the Hispanic society and her undying assistance as a real estate agent and humanitarian in helping the impoverished finding affordable housing. Above all, I know she will always be the personification of a caring, protective, and loving mother. Son, at 82 years old, I am still in love with your mom as much as the first day I met her. Please watch out for her."

"Dad, are you really joyful, as you say you are, knowing your life is ending?"

"Son, remember, we can't control our circumstances or control what other people do. We can only control our own attitude. This is where the power lies. You see, I have been freed from the things that have bound me to this world."

"Dad, how were you freed?"

"When I found out I only had six to 12 months to live, I wasn't bothered that your mother had to work late, or that the yard was not in tip-top shape. The knowledge of knowing you will die within a time period is initially shocking, but, in due course, it releases you from being bothered by the mundane. You see, Son, life is viewed differently with a disparate attitude. With this new perspective, you cease to be stressed in traffic, in the long lines at the grocery store, and even when family or workers get under your skin. This new outlook allows one to rise above the negativity and develop an appreciation for every moment as a life lesson, which ultimately serves us to become one with God."

"How do you rise above it, Dad?"

"It is in keeping your human life in perspective. We will not always be here. You too will die someday, Son, as will your mom, sisters, brother, and myself. The way to rise above it is to remember that each day is a gift from God, and I see that now. Son, I want you and everyone else to know what I have been told by God. He guides every step of our lives and gives us our lives to live in joy. Yet, it is up to each of us to embrace this promise from God by living each day in joy, which is truly peace. I had a year to live in total joy and peace, and I do not regret one day. It is a choice. I chose to be a victor and not a victim."

"Dad, what should I do and not do?"

"First of all, find out what is taking your joy. Identify those things that aggravate you and then take a conscious approach to change those things that are making you anxious in those areas. People go year after year letting the same things bother them. Every time they get caught in traffic they react the same way. When your mom did certain things or came home from work frustrated, it annoyed me and soured my day. Do what you have always done, and get what you have always gotten. Do what you have always done, differently, and watch the changes commence in your life. You see, being unhappy merely means that you are letting exasperating situations steal your joy, like living anxious, discontent, discouraged, and dispirited. You can choose to be bitter or better. It is always about the choice.

"Son, God assures us that this earthly life can be joyful or disappointing. We cannot wish it away or pray it all away. It is a part of life. What we have to do is to learn to handle it the right way. Son, it is very freeing when you understand this principle. For me, the Bible was a manual that was left by God to teach us how to handle life as well as how to get back home. Once you understand what God wants us to know and what has always been in our hearts, you will learn you don't have to give away your joy or peace. You don't have to get upset if you couldn't make it on time to your son's football game, or you didn't have enough time to go to your sister's party. You will see that God was leading your steps by changing things around you. What you thought might be a bad choice, like having taken the wrong turn, is really the right turn. You will see at times that God was keeping you from harm or from more anxiety-producing elements, or even leading you into a situation where someone stranded needed your help. You see, at the end of that day, you may have not gotten home the way you wanted, but you got home the way God chose. This is where miracles occur my son. Please believe me. This is what I have been told. The choice is yours. Make it happen."

"Why are you telling me this now, Dad?"

"So you don't have to wake up one day telling yourself, 'I wasted all those years being stressed at my job, years of being annoyed or frustrated by people, and years of dreading cleaning the house or mowing the lawn.' If you change your approach and believe that God is directing your steps to a place that is exactly where you are suppose to be, then you will come back to that place of peace. You will not only enjoy your life more, God will pour out his blessings and favor, and you will live the life of victory his has in store for you."

"Dad, I definitely want to live in joy and not be forced to give my joy away. I want God to lead my steps, as I know his way is always the right way. I will teach this to my children and to people who I meet."

"I am so glad my son. I will always be guiding you from the other side. Don't worry."

"Dad, when you said that's what 'they' told you, who is they?"

"You know, the men that visited me and have continued to visit me. You have written about these types of beings in your book and have spent your life studying it."

"So you read my book, Dad?"

"Yes. Initially I wasn't quite sure I truly believed in this angel bit at the end of life and that they would help me cross over."

"Why didn't you believe, Dad?"

"Well I guess I was fearful of dying, and I didn't want to think about it at all. I was afraid of death being nothingness, and I would lose all of you and your mom forever. I did want to believe in God, and I thought I did, but, as I got older, the fear of death stole my relationship with God and the joy that came with it. I was totally wrong, Son. Everything your patients have seen, I have seen. The feelings of joy, exhilaration, and freedom they felt, I feel. The angels are beautiful and the auras around God's creations are spectacular. For the first time, I know what you meant when you spoke about oneness. I see that what shines from the trees, the house, and our bodies is the same color. The difference is that people have a circular shimmering light in the center of their chest. I believe that is the soul."

"Are you seeing your parents, Dad? Jesus? Mary? Children?"

"Yes, I have seen my mother, father, and brother, and they are so happy and youthful-looking, just the way your patients mention. I have not seen Jesus or Mary as of yet, but I know I will. When the hospice nurse arrived tonight, she came in with a young girl around 5 years old with black hair and blue eyes, wearing a red-checkered dress. She was very excited when she saw me, and began to jump all over. When I asked if that was her daughter, she said there was no one in the room and she did not have a child. When the nurse departed, the child stayed, and is still here as we speak."

"What does she want? Who do you think she is?"

"She just smiles and caresses me, but doesn't talk. I am not sure who she is, but the thought that did enter my mind was that she was the child your mother and I lost before birth. I am not sure. I do feel a connection with her. Much like the connection I have with you and your siblings."

"Have you said anything to her?"

"I have asked her who she is and what she wants, but no response. I do feel, though, that I know her and that she is here to help me. I told her I loved her, and she hugged me."

"Wow, Dad. You are so blessed. I don't know what to say."

"Just say you will get here soon, so I can see you and hug you. I also want you to be my hospice doctor. I would not have anyone else care for me, because I know your compassion for others exceeds the compassion for yourself."

"Oh Dad, I love you so much. I would be honored to help you transition to God. I will be their real soon. Ana, Carmen, and Hector will arrive tomorrow."

When I arrived in Brownsville almost eight hours later, I kissed and hugged my mom, who was trying to be really strong, and walked directly to my father's bedroom. There he was, trying to walk from the bathroom to the bed, huffing and puffing from the increasing fluid in his lungs from the aortic stenosis—induced heart failure. "Dad, let me help you to bed," I asked. As we walked to the hospital bed, which he wanted placed alongside the floor-to-ceiling windows overlooking the beautifully landscaped foliage of the backyard, he looked at me and said, "I love you." That was unusual for my dad to say, as he was a stoic military man. I looked back and eagerly told him I also loved him. After getting him back into bed, he said he needed to rest a bit, but wanted to speak to me when he woke up. I covered him with a blanket, placed his oxygen mask on his face, and gave him a nebulized treatment of albuterol and ipratropium for his shortness of breath. This eased his rapid breathing to a point where he was able to sleep. My mom and I walked out of his room, and spent some time talking. I was careful not to tell my mom everything he had shared with me, as spouses of many years needed to be cared for with lots of love and understanding. I did not mention dad's terminal illness, but I did tell her that he was comfortable and that I would be here for the remainder of his time on earth. My mother was obviously comforted by this, and I saw her body relax. I said, "Mom, why don't you go to bed, and get some needed rest? I will watch Dad." My mother went to bed, and I stayed up waiting for my dad to wake up. Almost two hours later, I heard my father talking. As I walked into his room, I saw him reaching out to the right side of his bed like he was caressing someone's hair. "You are so beautiful. Thank you for being here for me and helping me find peace. Okay, I am ready, but I need to wait for the rest of my children to come, then I will go." At that moment, he pulled his arm back to his chest, and settled into his bed with a big smile.

By the next morning, the rest of my siblings showed up: my sister from San Francisco, my brother from Guadalajara, Mexico, and my other sister from Mexico City. All of us had a chance to talk to our father, and everyone was able to forgive each others' sins, allowing my dad to leave this world with a clean soul and a sense of closure that his children would always help each other and their mom. This made my dad so joyful. He shared the stories of the angels and the girl with my sisters, but kept it from my mom. I am sure it was to protect her from undue pain of my journey back home. Now we were all laughing around my dad's bed, reminiscing about our recent trip on a Caribbean cruise, among our childhood experiences. My brother and I, who are jokesters, began imitating George Lopez and telling many of his jokes.

All of us were so happy. It was as though nothing was wrong. My dad was right: The reason we were joyful was because we chose to hold on to our joy and not give in to the idea of death. I will never forget Dad's final lesson he imparted to his family.

At that moment the hospice nurse entered to care for my dad overnight. We left the room so she could bathe him and give him his medicines. After she was done, we all walked in one more time, and said goodbye to my dad. Everyone stepped out except the hospice nurse and myself. Knowing my dad was ready to leave this world, I asked him a few more questions, wanting to know the was comfortable and to see if he needed anything.

"Dad, can I get you anything, or do something for you?"

"No, son, I have everything I would ever want. My family is here, and we have forgiven each other and have found peace and joy. I know now that your mom and all of you will be fine. Son, my mom, dad, brother, and six angels are in the room, along with Sarah, the little girl, an archangel I think, and they told me Jesus will come soon to take me back home. They are so beautiful. Don't ever worry about anything son. Heaven is real, and everything and everyone is totally loving and compassionate. I have a better understanding now of what life on Earth is about, and why it is the way it is today. But that is today. I know through a deep feeling that his plan is to change this pattern for the better. We will always be involved in helping souls move forward. There are billions and billions of souls that are planning to be born. Many of them will impact this world in ways that will bring freedom and peace to this world.

"You know, I can see your white to golden aura along with angel, the nurse. Both of you have such brilliance, and your soul is deep, deep blue to purple, and the nurse's is pink to gold. How magnificent and beautiful. The birds and butterflies I saw outside the window earlier today had little souls that were light blue. I was told that birds and butterflies exist to act as bodies that spirits can enter to catch the attention of their earthly loved ones. Most people are not aware of this, but they are still happy just to be able to be on the physical plane."

"Dad, I will never forget what you have taught me, and the loving discipline you gave me, and, above all, for being my father and allowing me to care for your body as your spirit's awe-inspiring journey is about to begin. I love you."

I kissed him and left the room to spend time with the rest of my family. Still reminiscing about our past, we were enthralled in a divine joy that oozed from every cell of our being and every object around us. Within minutes, the nurse walked out, and in reverence she said, "Your dad has gone with the angels." We ran to the room, and, in amazement, saw my dad smiling with his hands outreached on his lap. I knew Daddy was smiling and reaching forward to the foot of the bed to take hold of Jesus. We then felt a light warm breeze penetrate our souls, and I knew it was Daddy's true essence. He was finally free to soar eternally through the vast cosmos spreading joy wherever he went.

Doctor's Notes

The evening after my dad passed the lights and ceiling fan automatically turned on around the time of his death for three consecutive nights. The lights or fan had never turned on prior to that day and have not turned back on since that time. My dad had told me that, when he returned, it would be through electrical circuitry, birds, or butterflies. I am sure, as my mom was, that my dad had told us he was okay, by turning the lights on. This made my mom comfortable and at ease. My dad always paid the bills at the office next to their bedroom, and to this day my mom hears my dad in the office, shuffling as he walks while gently whispering her name. This did not scare my mother but, rather, brought her much consolation and solace.

Two or three months later, while I was visiting home hospice patients in San Antonio, I saw a gorgeous monarch on the door handle of my BMW. Almost immediately, I thought about my dad's comment regarding butterflies, so I said, "Is that you, Dad?" It would not move, even when I grabbed the handle and opened the door. The magnificent butterfly flew to the front windshield and flew away after the car began to move. As I arrived at my next home visit and walked out of the car, another (or the same?) monarch landed on my right shoulder. It stayed on my shoulder even while walking. This was phenomenal. Was this really my dad? Was it possible for spirits to enter another animal and control their actions? If so, then this could be my father. At that moment, I accepted the miraculous event for what I felt it was and said, "Thank you, Dad." I knew my dad left about 40 days after his death, because I stopped feeling the warmth that surrounded me when the butterfly left my shoulder. I felt that was my dad telling me he was ready to move on to learn more. I do know when he comes back, though, because I feel his secure warmth around my body, and feel that shimmering light within my chest that he spoke of, expand.

Twenty-four hours before his death, my dad said that two angels (who had human forms and radiated the brightest white and maroon to golden light), explained that his life review was to include learning more about love and peace, as these gifts were two of God's more important weapons. "Man's choice of weapons to fight tyranny, terrorism, and wars are polar opposites of God's way. Man would not know God's intention for each individual crisis that would develop, unless they truly believed in him and involved him in their total lives, and not just when it was convenient. I was told that if man did not seek God in their decision-making process to achieve enduring peace and love, man would always resort to the ways of Cain and Abel, and, ultimately, fail at achieving peace. Some of the new weapons make it easy to kill, as one no longer has to look into the eyes and soul of the other man."

My father continued and said, "Even though the Bible says that God said there would be wars and rumors of wars, it did not mean that he approved of them. He was merely stating a fact: Where man lived, one could be assured of wars and more wars. Jesus did not believe that war was the answer, even if one was in his or her right or being threatened. He did endow us with the involuntary reaction to protect ourselves, but he also endowed us with a higher and voluntary desire to seek peace. If one sought peace, he promised us we would find it, but only if we had the faith and trust in him to deliver. God understood this would be difficult for us, as we were endowed with the ego. He knew that one day man would choose a different way to seek peace, and that would be by seeking him first. This one beautiful angel with radiant golden-brown hair and an ivory/silvery flowing frock, named Esther, said that everyone would have the occasion to replay their wars in their minds and finally arrive at the solution to the crisis that culminated toward peace. Esther said that this way of understanding that peace was attainable through one method is terribly taxing to one's consciousness, but believing in God's forgiveness would deliver us from our self-conviction. Everyone moves forward, but at varying speeds and time. This could be something similar to your school system, where, in order to move forward to the next grade, one must pass the exams that test your understanding of the lessons. Some may have to repeat the seventh grade for 10,000 years, but eventually even that soul moves forward, and toward enlightenment or the true essence of God."

My dad explained that if everyone takes advantage of understanding and seeking the God within, and uses the trust found in him to guide us through the lessons of faith, hope, and love, then everyone will have moved light-years ahead toward illumination, and now within the essence of God. "This is heaven I saw before I died. It was saturated with self-forgiveness, self-love, acceptance of the forgiveness from God by believing in his son, then external forgiveness and love for all, with selfless acts of kindness, giving, and living a life where less is more. These attributes are already within everyone, and thus heaven has always been with us. All one has to do is awaken them by becoming aware of their higher self. This is what Jesus was trying to explain to his followers when he said, "Where two or more are gathered, there I am in their midst."

My dad said that Esther had so much incredible insight into the mechanics and consequences of war. She said that, even if one wins a war, the immediate and long-term effects would haunt everyone for generations. Ending—and not beginning—wars is the goal. Continuing wars and killing plants a seed of hatred every time somebody is killed or maimed. To achieve peace, man would have to find each seed and love it, until it changes or dies. Eventually, all remembrance of the pain and hatred inflicted by wars will be erased. For example, every time the United States bombs Iraq or Afghanistan, I am sure some innocent civilians are killed, and those family members or citizens will live to hate and seek vengeance on a level that humans have never experienced. Their need for vengeance, similar to ours, is placed on God's lap. Yet, God does not exact retribution on the way our religious leaders taught us. Man exacts his own vengeance.

I asked my father if Esther mentioned whether God would destroy the Earth, as it is mentioned in the Bible, to eliminate evil. What he learned was that our loving God never decided to drown people who did not listen to him, and he would never do it by fire or any other method. This was hypocrisy on God's part. He could kill us, but we were to follow his commandment of "Thou shalt not kill." The flood did occur, but only in the East regions. This was the Earth's reaction to sudden temperature changes, and God was aware of this impending disaster, so he tried to save his people by speaking to them and telling them how to save themselves. He was trying to save us, not kill us. The thing was that most people would not listen or were not spiritually awakened to understand what they were hearing.

Man said if there is a fire in the future, then God is warning us to help us, not to condemn us or force us into his ways. This concept goes against his whole reason for creating Man and free will. Because God is perfection and love, and knows the number of hairs on our head, then he knew that we would be sinners and never be able to reach peace and salvation alone. That is why his plan included sending his son, who is God in human form, to teach us the way to peace, love, and salvation. He did not promise we would not suffer. In fact, he said he would suffer with us, because he lived in us. He was not sitting on a throne watching us go through sorrow and pain. His accomplishments as a man more than 2,000 years ago have made us victorious. All we have to do to win is freely acknowledge and accept our victory.

The victor is deep within everyone, and is waiting to have a loving relationship. He is waiting to carry us across the finish line. He promised his undying love and support through all our lessons, until such time that we would reach a level of eternally undying and never-changing love. He wants us to try to never give up on peace and love. It may cost our earthly life, but it will never, ever take our eternal soul. It is this part of us that will never die. Once we realize this fact, we will not fear death or fear itself.

The angels told my dad that the only way peace will manifest itself in this world one day is through the eradication of the human instinctual dark side. How this will occur is questionable to humans, but clear to all in the spiritual realm. It may be through a rapid metamorphosis of our caterpillar-DNA to the butterfly-DNA, if you will, which represents final freedom from our imprisoned souls, or the human form of God, which will return and allow the ego to wither away. Remember: The ego is essentially our weaker or sinful side. My dad mentioned that God's angels are concerned with the fact that we have unknowingly created God into our image and man has put a spin on the Bible's messages. God and Jesus are total loving beings and do not have one mean atom in their essence. He told me, "What I found interesting, Son, was that the angels said God's coming would be exactly as God said it, but not the way the prophets translated it. The angels would not comment on this statement any further except that we would not be disappointed."

God talks about total unification of our brothers and sisters on this plane, as well as to those he also created throughout the universe and parallel worlds. He clearly states this in many sacred texts, including Ephesians. It is vital for this entanglement of collective thoughts to occur (through group meditation or prayer), as this is the only way to the paradigm of our new peaceful and loving way of life. Collective prayer can and will create rapid and sustained reactions that will usher in this era of peace and love. Remember that another name for love is God. So one can say

God will return physically and spiritually to this world when critical mass of love and peace is achieved. For now, he resides in each and every one of us.

God could not be clearer about our quantum connection.

The way karma and dharma occur is scientifically explained through this law as well. Just remember that whatever you do to someone else, good or bad, will have an immediate cause and effect not only on that person, but also on you and the entire universe. How do we protect ourselves from people's projection of bad will? Through interference of those negative thoughts from reaching their intended target. This interference is created through prayer or meditation. Preferably, prayer by two or more.

The only ways to beat the sinister darkness within ourselves is through the daily connection of our consciousness with God, and then entangling oneself with our prayer partners, family, friends, and the world. What we ask God is simple: for his will to be done and for repentance of our dark ways through understanding why they exist.

One of the last angelic messages given to my dad was as follows: "Every human soul is destined to appreciate this vast comprehension, but only with the guidance of our Teacher."

2 The Angel's Wife

When Mary suddenly lost her husband from a heart attack, she was completely lost and grief-stricken. Worried about her, I called that same evening to chat. When she answered the phone, I thought I had the wrong number, because the lady who answered sounded elated and extremely joyful. I hesitated for a moment, after which she recognized my voice and commented, "Dr. John, so glad to hear your voice. Are you doing okay? If not I can come over to take care of you."

I answered, "Mary, of course I'm okay. Thank you for your concern. I was calling to make sure you were fine." At this point I really thought that she had either taken an overdose of her mood-elevating medicine or was having an unusual psychotic break. "Mary, why are you so happy and full of joyful laughter?"

"Well, I don't want you to think I am crazy, Dr. Lerma. When I arrived from the funeral this evening, I entered the bedroom sobbing, and, as I went to lie on the bed, a bright, white, and pulsating light coming from the edge of the bed gently nudged me. I was not frightened, Dr. Lerma. In fact, I was totally comforted and loved by it. Within seconds, the light contracted to the shape of a human being and then, as it defined itself, I saw my dead husband, Bill. At least it looked like him and sounded like him when he spoke to me. Do you believe me Dr. John?" Mary replied.

"Of course I do. I have had many spouses tell me they usually have these type of experiences shortly after the death of their loved one."

Mary was comforted by that knowledge and went on to tell me that "Bill looked like he was in his 30s and totally healed. He was wearing a beautiful white and blue shirt and the lower half was translucent. His aura was a vivid gold, and it encircled my entire being, making me feel warm, loved, forgiven, accepted, and without any physical or emotional discomfort. Bill explained that he would always protect and guide me as well as pray to God to heal me from my severe arthritis and advancing glaucoma. I am able to do this because of your faith and desire to connect with the next world and not the things of Earth."

I wondered for a moment if that's what it took to achieve heaven on Earth.

Bill showed Mary a glimpse of heaven and some of the specific things that one experienced soon after making the transition to heaven. She only told me that heaven was not like all the pictures we had seen on Christmas cards, in Christian books, and so forth. Heaven was much grander, but yet full of simplistic beauty. For her and her husband, their version was one of majestic mountains, loving wildlife, pristine rivers, and a deep passion to help souls throughout his universe understand the power of love and forgiveness. There is life everywhere! God knows no limit when he lovingly creates. Free will continues to exist in the next realm and is truly the best gift God gave us. In heaven, free will allows one to create along side God and he lights up when one of his souls uses it as it was intended for the first time. On Earth, it is quite limited, and is used to attain understanding and wisdom on how to find goodness within all things. With God, there are no ego-based energies, and thus, free will is now open to freely fashion itself. Bill told her that it is on Earth that we learn many things that we carry with us to heaven, including our imagination and dreams that we draw from to create. If one does not take time to read, experience, and think on Earth, then our view of heaven and our ability to shape our reality will be limited. Developing more experience will come from helping others in the world they know.

What Mary was telling me some how resonated deep within, and this knowledge has furthered my desire to grow in knowledge and wisdom from self-examination, unconditional love, suffering, random acts of kindness, and, above all, developing a personal relationship with our Creator.

"Dr. John, do you now understand my joyful demeanor?" Mary asked.

"Without a doubt, Mary. Without a doubt."

At her next visit with her ophthalmologist, she had Dr. Opstaruss call me to share the great news. It's as Bill had told her: Mary's glaucoma was gone. There could only be one explanation. It was a miracle!

3
Dying to See Angels

Death is no more than passing from one room to another. But there is a difference for me, you know, in that other room, I shall be able to see.

—Helen Keller

Sarah was only 10 years old when she heard her first sunrise on Easter Sunday as she walked up Villa della Conciliazione toward Piazza San Pietro in Rome. Sarah described it to me, as she waited to have her last chemotherapy session.

"I marveled at the multitude of loving sounds that Bernini's dramatic design was exuding. As I walked through the towering, ornate doors of St. Peter's Basilica, I was drawn by an alluring vibration toward the chapel to my right. What I was allowed to hear was beyond awe. The vibrations and frequencies, now a part of my entire being, were the remnant echoing sounds of sadness replaced by utter joy and exuberant love from the statue where Jesus was heard to be lying on his mother's lap after being crucified. I knew I was now standing in front of Michelangelo's most honored statue, the 'Pieta.' Feeling some unfamiliar loving force take hold of my hand, I took hold of my mother's and followed with total faith. I told my mom not to worry and to trust me, as there was an angel leading us to our next spiritual experience. As this comforting and protective spirit of God led me around this huge sanctuary of Christian religion toward the front of St. Peter's Church, I heard a gentle voice tell me, 'this is where God would like you to sit.'

"My mother, Bridget, told me this was cute, but this seating was reserved and we needed to move. By this time, it was essentially standing room only, so I persisted on remaining in the seats that were allotted to us by the angel. Dr. Lerma, by that time, just as my mother was about to take me by the hand to the back of the Basilica, I heard a familiar pulsating tone approach us and then a soft, loving voice asked my mom if there was a problem. The gentleman introduced himself as Father Delaney. In reverence, I told Father Delaney that my mother and I had come to Rome to visit the Basilica during Easter and to ask God to heal the affliction that caused my blindness. I hesitated to tell this kind-hearted Catholic priest the rest of the story, because I was beginning to doubt myself, so I told him my mother and I were hoping to find a place to sit close to the altar.

"With with what sounded like warm smile on his face, Father Delaney told us not only could we could sit in the area where we originally were, but after the Mass, he would to take us to meet Pope John Paul II, and obtain his blessing. My mother and I were in utter disbelief at the set of circumstances that had transpired. My mother asked me if I could still hear or feel the angel that led us to these seats. I told my mother I could not hear or feel the angel, but I knew he was close by and would make himself known again real soon. As the angelic sound of cardinals and priests walked past me, I then heard a different, more glorious sound pass to my left. It was Pope John Paul II. Amazing warmth and healing power radiated from his hands as he blessed the crowd. Once again, I could make out sounds emanating from everything around the Basilica, both animate and inanimate, as if everything was glorifying God. The entire scene was surreal and astounding. Dr. Lerma, my mother pinched me and I pinched her, to make sure we were not dreaming. Throughout the entire Papal Mass, I was sensing colors and images through sounds, from the relics and paintings inside the Basilica, as well as from the angels I knew were flying around the Sacristy.

"Once again, I felt someone holding my hand, but this time it was not leading me somewhere. It was merely holding my hand out of love. I knew it was the angel that had held my hand earlier that day. I smiled and asked under my breath what his name was. I distinctly heard Cherin. As Cherin began singing praises to God as he held my hand, so did I. It was difficult to make out the words he was singing, so I just made up my own. As I began to sing, I was almost certain that I heard Jesus descending just above me with a long reverberating sound of extraordinary colors of love and peace surrounding him and everyone in the church. That is probably why Cherin appeared to me at this time, as well as why he was singing with fervor. I remember never having felt this content and happy.

"At the end of Easter Mass, Cherin was still holding my hand, and he told me to sit and wait for Father Delaney. I told my mother the angel was back, and wanted us to wait for the priest to return. By this time, my mother was so immersed in the God incidents as well as the joyous feeling from being present at a Papal Mass, that she sat down without question. As expected, Father Delaney returned and thanked us for waiting. He told us to follow him along with several other children and parents as Pope John Paul II wanted to meet us and bless us individually and as a group. My mother and I were about to burst in anticipation of meeting our Holy Father. Cherin was still holding my hand and swinging it back and forward in what I am sure was complete joy. We were all taken to another room in St. Peter's Basilica, and asked to sit and wait for his Holiness, Pope John Paul II. I recall the room being much smaller, but equally as warm and loving, and now saturated with the most beautiful sounds and vibrations of desire and hope that were felt to be piercing my very heart and soul. I knew these sounds quite well, and knew they were radiating from the children and their parents. I, too, held hope to be able to see again, as the little girl next to me held hope to be cured from her bone cancer. I was feeling everyone's illness, pain, and hope. I didn't understand it, Dr. Lerma, and maybe I was not supposed to, but, I know I was to comprehend the meaning of hope. That is why all of us were here. Dr. Lerma, what happened next exceeded all of my expectations as well as my mother's, and I am sure all the other children and their parents.

"Cherin whispered in my ear that the Holy Father was coming, so he took my hand and told me to stand. All the other children must have had their own angel, as my mother told me we all appeared to be standing up in unison and without a formal announcement from Father Delaney. Mesmerized as to why we stood up, I knew he was aware that there was something greater than him coordinating this most glorious occasion. At the moment our Holy Father walked in, I began to hear the sound of several angels singing on either side of me. Cherin told me I was hearing all the guardian angels singing in reverence of the Pope. 'I so wish I could see them singing as well as the faces of all the children as our Holiness entered,' Sarah replied.

"The Pope greeted all of us, and with immense compassion and empathy, he gently held me and placed my head on his chest over his heart, and just loved me. As tears began to flow down my face, I remember he gently placed a finger on my cheek and let one tear roll onto his finger. He then whispered into my ear, 'My child, this teardrop holds the faith needed to heal you in ways you can not imagine. God has sent an angel to guard you and guide you as you prepare to glorify him through a miraculous life. You will help many come to believe in an all-loving God. Sarah, like you, I could be healed from my ailments, but we are being asked to view suffering for its strength and not its weakness. You see, Sarah, Jesus' plan is to bring all souls back home, but he needs the empowering innocence of children and their willful suffering to engender his design. Pray for understanding and wisdom my child.'

"Dr. Lerma, I guess you know the choice I made. When our Holy Father had finished talking to everyone, the spirited energy in the room was almost palpable. Simultaneously, I heard the angels singing the following words, 'Glory, glory Hallelujah. Glory, glory Hallelujah. Glory, glory Hallelujah. His truth keeps marching on.'

"Dr. Lerma, I was sure that most of the children around me heard the angels singing, since most were humming the tune I was hearing. Within seconds, I heard Pope John Paul II singing and then Father Delaney. The rest of us joined in as best as we could. I was in ecstasy as I heard the words echoing throughout the Basilica. It was simply enchanting. I would find out years later that this song was one of Jesus' favorites.

"As we walked out of the Basilica, the sun was now setting, and I was sure I could hear its vibrations as well as a string of harmonious angelic tones." Sarah went on to describe how the notes crescendoed into a celebratory symphonic masterpiece that symbolized the eternal reunion of God, Jesus, and all his souls. I could see God's plan as Pope John Paul II told me I would. Yes,

I could see for the first time in my life; not with my eyes, but with the frequency made from the vast colors, sights, and sounds as only God could create. It was then that I completely and with total love, accepted my role in God's plan."

I was in complete awe at what Sarah had shared. I tried so hard keep the tears from building up in my eyes, but I could not. How could anyone? I had heard so many amazing stories, but never one that touched my heart and soul to the extent this one did. "Dr. Lerma, I know my time is nearing, so please stop all remaining chemotherapy and radiation treatments. I want to be alert as possible the last few weeks of my life, as I want to see God's angels with my eyes. Cherin came back last night and told me he and so many other angels, as well as my parents, would be coming soon to present a gift from God. I think I know what it is Dr. Lerma. Do you?"

"Absolutely. In fact, please don't laugh when you see my gray hair." Sarah smiled and laughed almost uncontrollably. Listening to her laughter thrilled me to no end.

It was almost three weeks until Easter and Sarah's last chemotherapy had been given, as she had desired. Her oncologist had agreed to stop treatment as her disease process had advanced so rapidly. It was as if Sarah knew her cancer had spread before we did. The malignancy was now invading her brain, liver, lung, and bone marrow with subsequent depletion of white cells, red cells, and platelets. How Sarah was still able to converse and recall events was astonishing to say the least, not to mention how she was able to maintain such a beautiful and loving demeanor throughout her journey of blindness and cancer.

"Dr. Lerma, one of the good things about being blind and developing an aggressive form of cancer is that I do not have to see myself the way others see me, or see themselves; young or old, thin or fat, ugly or beautiful, short or tall, healthy or ill. I will always see myself the way my heart and not my eyes taught me to see myself, which is with total love."

After Sarah's chemotherapy treatment, she was transferred back to her room, where we continued our conversation. She expanded on her family history and began by telling me that she was born blind as a result of atrophic optic nerves, a very rare condition only affecting one in 100,000 newborns, where the nerves responsible for carrying objects seen to the occipital cortex are not fully developed. Sarah explained that she had no concept of colors, light, or darkness. Her dreams were not visual in nature. Instead, they were composed of her four remaining senses, which were smell, taste, hearing, and touch. She spoke of being able to understand shapes through touch, taste, and sounds, but was unable to discern color in any form. Since the age of 5, she learned to hear colors, such as the light of the sun rising and setting.

She functioned well throughout her life, remaining active in school and church, until the age of 29, at which point she was diagnosed with an aggressive form of breast cancer. As an only child, Sarah lived with her loving parents, never married, and had no children. She never worried about living alone, as she always felt she would die before her parents. However, this feeling would not be realized. Both her parents would die from cancer as she celebrated her 26th birthday. Sarah described her ensuing depression, as her life had been turned inside out. It was during this time of suffering that Sarah began to understand the meaning of the words Pope John Paul had whispered to her as a child. She understood that her suffering was bringing her closer to God, and he was all she would think about during her illness. The relationship she developed with her Creator had now flourished and empowered her with the ability to self-heal. "Pope John Paul was right: The one single teardrop that fell from my cheek removed the pain, and for a short period of time healed the surrounding cancerous skin, though it was up to me if I wanted to accept the healing of my entire cancer. Once I knew the power of healing existed, I decided to suffer joyfully for those people far from God. Dr. Lerma, I cannot explain how suffering actually helps others. All I know is that it's faith that makes it happen. If I die, I will be able to help an immeasurable number of souls from heaven, where you can be in infinite places at once accomplishing infinite tasks at once. Remember, Dr. Lerma, that working side by side with human souls is the key to ushering in God's plan, as well as bringing joy and peace to our earthly lives. All one has to do is communicate, listen, and open oneself to goodness, kindness, compassion, and forgiveness. It feels so right to be a part of God's plan in helping return. We are so important to God that he will not stop until his loving design is manifested."

I had goose bumps as I reflected on Sarah's divinely inspired words. What she expressed resonated deep within my essence.

Sarah fell asleep when she finished talking. I stood up and walked over to her hospital bed, kissed her on her forehead, and whispered in her right ear that she "fly with the angels anywhere her heart desired." I asked the nurses at the hospice unit to take the entire collection of brightly colored stuffed animals and place them on her bed and around her pillow. I also had the nurses place a coloring book and crayons on the table over her bed, in hopes that, if Sarah was able to see before transitioning, she would use the appropriate colors to draw the angels, her parents, and anything else she saw. I had not told Sarah about my plan because I did not want to affect the outcome of my informal study. There was no doubt in my mind that with all Sarah had witnessed as a child, she would come to see the glory of God as she left her body.

Three days later, I arrived at the unit around 7 a.m., and as I walked into Sarah's room I found that the pad had been opened and several markings resembling the letter, A, L, E, and S had been written. Sarah was sleeping at the time, so I went and asked the nurses if they knew who might have written the letters. All four staff members denied writing the note, and Sarah had not had visitors. The night shift nurses did recall that around four in the morning, Sarah woke up, asked for some water, and fell back asleep. Thirty minutes later, the nurses remember hearing Sarah speaking to someone in the room. When they checked, there was no one present, except Sarah, and she was sitting up looking to the right corner of the room. She continued talking peacefully, so the nurses walked out and left the door open. The nurses did not recall much of what was said except that she kept repeating, "It's so pretty, Mom. It's so pretty."

When I walked back to the room, the nurse's followed to see the writing. All agreed the writing looked like the letters, A, L, E, and S. One of the nurses said she must have been trying to write the word *angel*, but was missing the letter *n* and *g*. When Sarah awoke, the nurses called me. I walked in Sarah's room and began the following dialogue.

"Hi, Sarah. I heard you had a peaceful night. By the way, did you use the pad I left on the table by your bed to write something down last night?"

"Yes, Dr. Lerma. I smelled the familiar smell of crayons close to me, so I felt around and found them. You see, I had heard the nurses talk about a pad and color you had left on the table, so after the vision of Cherin and my mom, I wanted to write down the word *angels*. I have studied fiercely in the past to be able to write. I gave it up since it was too difficult and technology made it easier to use the computer. I was writing it for you Dr. Lerma. Well, now you will definitely know when I get my vision, as my penmanship will be better than your doctor writing."

(Sarah and I laughed at her funny comment.)

"Did the nurses talk about my handwriting?"

"I am not going to say."

"Don't worry, Sarah. I know the nurses can't keep secrets."
(Sarah laughs.)

"I must agree with that. I have great hearing, and I think they forget."

"So, tell me about the angels, Sarah."

"Well, there was something different in the vibrations of the room last night. It was very similar to the sounds and vibrations I heard and felt when I was at St. Peter's Basilica in Rome. After a few minutes, I heard Cherin and four other angels. They were very comforting, so I was able to feel their feather's brushing up against my body and face. I remember they smelled like roses, which I love. Music also seemed to follow them, much like what I experienced in Rome. These sounds were much more engaging and full of the same ingredients of the music I heard at the Basilica, being love, peace, hope, joy, and forgiveness. I guess these gifts and attributes have their own frequencies. A beautifully, soft, loving voice then came through the music. It was from a woman. She took my hand, placed it on her heart, and said: 'Sarah, you will see with your eyes before you return home. However, we need to prepare your mind and cells to be able to respond to what it sees without displeasure and confusion. With your hand over my heart, I am facilitating these actions. What would normally take weeks to months will only take seconds to hours.'

"Who are you? Were you the mother on the statue I stood in front of while in Rome? You must be Mary, Mother of God."

Angelic woman: "I am the woman you saw on the statue when you visited Rome."

"You mean you are Mary. The mother of Jesus Christ?"

Angelic woman: "Yes, I am, dear. You invited the angels and me into your heart and soul long ago, and we have been waiting to make ourselves known to you. You have done well, my dear. Many have been saved because of your selfless actions, and now God has many gifts for you; the first being sight of the world you will be leaving. The next has been made known to you years ago. We are here to guide you back home where you will be with your mother, father, and friends. So much more is waiting for you, my dear."

"What is waiting for me, Mary?" I asked.

Mary: "Only God can tell you, but know this, my dear: It is beyond anything your heart could ever imagine, or all the souls could ever create. It will not entail pain or suffering. Sarah, remember this and pass it on to those that are caring for you. Understand that one does not need to see with one's eyes to be able to live on Earth, to have a family, a job, enjoy life, and have a dream. Having sight is the one human sense that is so rewarding if used correctly, but treacherous as it can steer one in the wrong direction."

"Mary, before you leave, could you tell me what I will see when I am given the gift of sight?"

Mary: "Like I said earlier, you will see your parents, the multitude of angels, Jesus, many other spirits, and myself. You will initially see your soul as God formed it. You will see your acknowledgment in its role for your Father's loving plan in reuniting all souls. You will also see the birth of the universe, the birth of your world, the birth of life, and finally your birth. The images will be soft and obscure at first, but will progressively brighten as your mind connects the new pictures and the previous images created by your functioning senses of sound, taste, smell, and touch.

"We must now leave, Sarah. We love you with the love of God himself. You will begin to see slowly through the next few weeks. Pray for all the souls around you and throughout God's Creation, so that they will be in line with the will of the Father of Love, Forgiveness, and Peace."

"I felt them hug and kiss me, like you kissed me the other night. (Yes, Dr. Lerma. I was not totally asleep.)"

Sarah was quite fatigued by the time we finished talking, so she ate her breakfast and fell asleep.

Despite her disease progression, Sarah felt no significant pain.

She never complained of anxiety or showed signs of depression, and as a result, was not placed on psychotropics, which are usually sedating. She was adamant about being as alert as possible throughout her last days on this planet, as she wanted to be able to appreciate the gift God had promised her years ago. However, due to her decrease in oral intake, Sarah did agree to hydration via subcutaneous fluids, specifically Dextrose 5 percent with one half of the normal saline running at 75 cc/hour.

She tolerated the near 2 liters per day, as she was not in kidney failure, heart failure, and thus, pulmonary edema (fluid in her lungs). My goal was to keep Sarah as comfortable as possible by acknowledging and treating her spiritual, emotional, interpersonal, and physical pain. With her pain level now at 0–2/10, 10 being the worst, thirst at 0/10, anxiety at 0/10, depressive symptoms at 0/10, pulse at 90 (55–100 is normal) and a stable blood pressure of 110/50 (<120/80 normal), temperature at 98 degrees oral (98.6 oral is normal), respiratory rate of 18 (12–18 normal), and adequate urine output, I was absolutely certain that she was peaceful.

Sarah did share with me that, every time the angels appeared, her pain and mental distressing symptoms disappeared. Sarah explained, "Since the angels have been present every day, I have had no physical or emotional pain. I have learned that, to experience no pain, every individual must trigger the process of soul-detachment from the physical body, by willing the first loving spiritual being into our mind, body, and soul. The more spirits from God that appear, the faster the detachment and the greater the comfort. Now, if one chooses to deny God's initial preparatory spirit into their mind, body, and soul, then the soul-detachment process fails to be triggered, and one is left to perceive pain in its totality. Dr. Lerma, this information, if shared, may bring comfort to countless ill patients."

I commented to Sarah that several patients had mentioned that the first spirit or angel seen was usually standing quietly at the entrance to their room and lasted less than five seconds. They would ultimately enter when the patient willed them in, either verbally or through thought. No one had ever told me about the pain-relieving properties these visitations provided. Thank you for sharing this information, Sarah.

For the next two weeks, Sarah continued to decline, but was remarkably alert and comfortable. She had begun to show signs of organ malfunction, including her kidneys and liver. I decreased her fluid rate to 40cc/hour, or about 1 liter per day.

Her vitals remained quite stable despite her failing organs. (This is not unusual during the dying process.) During these two weeks, Sarah was now gaining sight and was seeing the angels on a daily basis, but only for seconds to minutes at a time. When I asked Sarah if she could see shadows or myself, she looked directly at me and then winked. I felt she was deflecting the answer because she wanted to wait until Easter to share her experiences and lessons with me. I knew Sarah and the angels had things under control. My job was now clearly defined: to keep her physically comfortable and alert.

It was now the Saturday before Easter, and with Sarah's physical status now declining rapidly, she expressed with avidity the need to speak with me. When the nurses called to tell me what Sarah had said, I immediately knew in my heart that she was nearing death. I quickly finished my hospital rounds and hurried to the hospice unit. To my surprise, she was looking very peaceful, but more pallid than earlier that day. Her urine output had decreased significantly, so I stopped her intravenous fluids, as I did not want to overload her lungs and worsen her oxygenation in the process.

As I reached across the bed to stop the flow of parenteral fluids, Sarah slowly lifted her hand, touched my face, and, with a tear rolling down her cheek, she said, "Dr. Lerma, please don't worry. You have done all you can to comfort me, and, for this and more, I will never forget you. My time has come to meet the Almighty. Gosh, Dr. Lerma, I have a case of the butterflies."

When I began to think about how I would feel if I was about to meet my Creator, my tummy began to feel excitable as well. I guess the spiritual relationship I had developed with Sarah had allowed me to connect with some of Sarah's most mystical feelings. I felt so honored. At that moment, Sarah looked directly into my eyes, as if she could see me, and urged my staff and me to continue sharing the gift of compassion, kindness, and love to those that God brought before us. Please pursue this ministry with intense passion until such day when God, his angels, your family, and myself return to carry you back home." Wiping away my tears, I relayed my love to Sarah and then asked the following questions.

"Sarah, can you see me now?"

"Yes, I can see, but still somewhat blurry. In fact, I began to gain sight few days ago, so I used the pad and crayons to draw something for you."

"Sarah, what did you draw?"

"It is a picture of me, Dr. Lerma. I used the mirror in the bedside table to look at myself, and decided what a better gift than how I see myself as I am about to meet God."

When Sarah showed me the drawing, I was in total shock as to what I saw. The drawing was very similar to Sarah, but more impressive were the accuracy of the colors chosen. She used the blue, pink, yellow, and red crayons accurately to denote her blue eyes, pink nightgown, and blonde hair. She also drew a large smile. Incredible. I wondered if my colleagues would believe that Sarah drew this picture. Probably not, but all that truly mattered was that Sarah, the nurses, and I knew the truth.

"Dr. Lerma, I have so much to tell you. I have learned so much more since I have been cured from my blindness. Feel free to tell others what I am about to share with you."

"First of all, let me start by telling you that I only see a few gray hairs on your spiked hair, Dr. Lerma. You actually look a lot younger than I had imagined. Listen to me; I am speaking like I have seen all my life. That's so funny. At any rate, I thought you would be this older, wise man using a walker or cane. Just kidding, Dr. Lerma."

"My spirit or soul is now at its highest energy, and my physical body, as you can see, is almost at its lowest point." This is of interest because most medical doctors view that the physical body and our spiritual essence are one in the same, and, as such, they believe both decline simultaneously. Most of my patients that are within hours from death exhibit a highly articulate thought and compassionate process, as opposed to a physical body that can no longer feed itself or move. If the physical body and our higher consciousness are one, then most, if not all, of my patients would not be able to speak or reason days to weeks before their transition. Most scientists believe that our consciousness and sub-consciousness is connected to the body for energy, and when the body weakens or dies, so does the mind.

"Why are terminally ill patients still witty, logical, emotional, loving, caring, forgiving, and still recall things in an instant, when their body is less than 100 pounds with multi-system organ failure? One would think that their mind would be very weak and confused, instead of being so alert. The strength their mind is exhibiting would likely be connected to a healthy and energized body. Where are they obtaining the energy for such clear mentation? Their higher self, higher consciousness, or soul is obviously connected to another power source. It is this other power source, if you will, that I want to tell you about, Dr. Lerma.

"I began to fully see as of yesterday. By the way, I love your light blue shirt, black slacks, leather belt, and your spiked hair. Dr. Lerma, you are too funny. Such a hip doctor caring for the terminally ill. Oh well. Maybe you should be working in a trendy L.A. or South Beach hospice. Again, just kidding. I love you just the way you are, Dr. Lerma."

"Sarah, could you tell me if there are angels around us now, and, if so, what they look like?"

"I feel totally energized and joyful, because there are so many angels around me. Each one is different. That's sort of cool. I would say their heights range from 4 feet to more than 10 feet, as the taller ones appear to be extending past the ceiling, which I think is 10 feet. Some have long blond hair, others short dark hair, and most of their eyes are blue, with a few of the taller ones having light brown to hazel-looking eyes. Their attire, if you will, consists of long, flowing robes, which seems to be silk-like in texture and snow white in color. None of the ones that are present have feathered wings; however, I am told that they do exist. The angels around us at this time appear to be floating in mid-air, and, as they enter and leave our dimension, they evoke an immensely bright light, which leaves a form of static electricity throughout the room. I wish you could see them, Dr. Lerma."

"Have you seen your parents? Do they look younger?"

"I saw them a few days ago and was told they would return tonight to guide me back home. They looked to be in their late 20s to early 30s, healthy, and extremely happy and content."

"Do you know anything about the gift God is going to give you?"

"I thought it was my sight, but the angels told me it's something else. You know something, Dr. Lerma? Some of the angels are really jokesters, and laugh a lot. They like it when we laugh. They say it is really healing and a sign of innocence, joy, compassion, and healing. Comedians are said to be inspired by angels, but many veer toward using the gift with negativity. Jesus loves to laugh, and wants us to learn to laugh effortlessly and frequently."

I could notice that Sarah was growing tired, but still comfortable, so I told her I wanted her to get some rest and we would continue our discussion tomorrow. I left Sarah late that evening filled with love, joy, laughter, and forgiveness, and for that I would always be grateful.

It was now Easter Sunday, around 4 a.m., when my phone awakened me. I was in a deep sleep and having a flying dream where my three children, Mark, Daniella, Arianna, and I were laughing uncontrollably as we proceeded to cover the White House with purple toilet paper. I continued laughing even after I woke up. I've always loved those kinds of dreams. The funny thing is that my kids and I would probably do something like that given the opportunity.

Sarah's nurse was calling to tell me that she had passed away peacefully with a smile on her face at 3:55 a.m. The nurse told me the following: "After you left last night, Dr. Lerma, Sarah and I spoke a bit as I washed her hair. In that conversation she said she wanted me to write a message for you so you would never forget her and the gift. "Dr. Lerma, I am very tired now, and because you knew I would be gone before your hospital rounds, I wanted to tell you that Jesus was here the whole time you and I were talking about the angels. He was sitting next to you and his energy was what gave us both total peace and comfort. The gift was on the other side of the bed, and his name was John. Yes, John Paul II. He showed me my tears that were still on his fingers and palms from my visit to Rome. When he rubbed them on my eyes, I was able to see infinitely more. I was looking at the kingdom of God. It was so worth it."

I thanked the nurse for taking time to write her message down and for loving her. We were her only family on Earth. I will never forget this loving and virtuous soul who chose to die to see angels.

Doctor's Notes

Sarah's List of Messages She Received From the Angels

1. Innocent laughter places one in a state of mind that radiates joy, acceptance, and appreciation, and calls out to us no matter how far we are, because of the law of attraction, where like attracts like.

2. On Earth, like attracts like and the opposite is true, so be careful. Negativity, such as hatred, anxiety, irritation, and doubt, does not send out the frequency to attract the angels. By working on getting to know oneself—your whole self, that is—one can determine the triggers for those negative traits,

choose to avoid them, and eventually learn to draw out the positive, such as laughter, joy, love.

3. Get to know and listen to your intuition. This hunch or intuitive feeling emanates from the solar plexus region. This is a great gift given to us by God, but most do not acknowledge it or use it. It is in this region that our connection to God, who knows and tells us the best of everything, exists. It is never wrong.

4. Always cultivate an enduring sense of gratitude. Be grateful for all God has given us and will give us. This type of thought process is positive, and positive begets positive. Look for positive in every moment and be proactive in this area.

5. Make time to have fun.

6. The more positive one is, the more God's spirits and angels will visit and joyfully make one's life easier. So, remove yourselves from any negativity, stressful situations, and anxiety to using forgiveness, understanding, wisdom, and love. Remember: Forgiveness and love are positive attributes, so using them also summons the angels in large numbers. Just merely trying to change, forgive, and love will allow the angels to move one toward healing and joy. It may take some time, but never lose faith or falter. If you do, know that Jesus walks wherever

he wants, including to the negative and positive, in order to save his children. God will never abandon you. He will still want you to change through the use of free will and it will be tough, but he will be by your side all the way. He will never stop loving all his souls. This is important to understand, as believing anything different will keep us from experiencing God.

Research Related to Blind Patients and NDEs:

It was interesting to find out about Dr. Kenneth Ring, a professor of psychology at the University of Connecticut, who carried out researched involving blind patients that had a near-death experience. Dr. Ring reported that almost 80 percent of these patients, some blind from birth and others after birth, maintained that they had been able to see while having a near-death experience. The incredible part was that many of these people had been blind from birth, similar to Sarah, and did not have any idea what having vision was like. They had absolutely no concept of what colors were, including black or darkness, but they did have dreams that were much like what they visualized the world through and that was through their remaining senses of hearing, smell, taste, and touch.

During these patients' near-death experiences (NDEs), they described floating out of their body and viewing their body as well as the people and environment around them. Some reported being pulled upward and through a dark tunnel with a bright, white light at the end, with God, angels, and formally at the end. It was usually at this point that these patients either negotiated to return to their body, or were told by spiritual beings that it was not their time to go through the light. When these people returned, their lives were usually changed in a very profound and meaningful way. Many report focusing on attributes such as love, forgiveness, joy, and kindness. So, the blind and the non-blind have almost identical experiences. When the blind are out of their body, they can see this world and the next. Interestingly, when those who are born blind recover their sight through a medical process, they report an initial period of disorientation, because it takes their minds some time to learn how to interpret what they are seeing. People who are blind from birth report difficulty relating to what they are seeing. Those who are not blind from birth, and had some memory of past sight, immediately recognize the return of vision.

Scientists believe that the blind can see during death, as they did not have total loss of brainstem function, and they still had mental functioning below an appreciable heart rate or blood pressure, which allowed them to see via dream-states, sensory-cueing, skin-based sight, and many other factors.

So how could he explain those patients who had no brainstem function but claimed to see their environment and specific objects, along with the medical staff's accurate description? This was not as easy, but scientists were sure that, if a person could see and hear things in his or her environment while clinically dead, then they were not dead. In all likelihood, it is very likely, to these scientists, that the body remains alive along with conscious-ness for some time after the heart and lungs stop functioning.

Doctors estimate that the body usually has more than seven minutes of brain-stem functioning with no appreciable oxygen or blood flow. For me, I have seen a few of my patients return after 20 minutes of no appreciable heart rate, blood pressure, and respiratory function, only to die later that day. They usually died later that day, claiming they needed to give a loving family mem-ber or friend closure. If no one is quite sure when death occurs, then it probably stands to reason that it might occur when the soul or one's higher self receives or gives the closure needed. After this process is carried out, it is my experience that the soul is at peace to leave the body permanently. This certainly gives a differ-ent twist to the importance of "closure."

The answer that fits most of the unexplained phenomena points to the most comforting explanation: There exists a soul, spirit, or higher self, that has the ability to visualize, without eyes, this world and the next. For Sarah, she had never seen any-thing in this world, but yet, at the end, she was actually seeing and locating the correct colors with which to draw. Besides sight, she also had knowledge of her time of death and was seeing an-gels while she was awake.

Sarah told me that the angels placed several small spheres of light into her eyes and these strongly energized spheres were able to bridge and bypass the atrophied optic nerve and travel through the original nerve to the occipital lobe. It is these intelligent nano-electromagnetic spheres that will one day allow a paralyzed person to walk, a demented patient to think clearly, or a person to see. Sarah said that this was the future of medicine. She remembers actually becoming one of these balls of light and traveling from her retina down the nerve and to the back of the brain where the visual cortex is located. She was bringing an image of herself as she looked into the mirror.

Of interest were the EEGs and PET scan I preformed on Sarah. I had two EEGs done during the last two weeks of life when she reported to be able to see. The EEG showed an unusual pattern, but similar to what I had previously seen with other non-blind, terminally ill patients. Could it be possible that there is a signature pattern on EEGs that would at least reveal, with some certainty, that the patient or subject is having visions of another dimension or non-locality? I am hoping to combine efforts with Dr. Peter Fenwick, a neuropsychiatrist in England, to begin a research project that attempts at defining pre-death experiences through EEG patterns.

With regard to Sarah's positron emission tomography (PET) scan, which is a test that measures important body functions such as blood flow, oxygen use, and sugar metabolism in organs such as the brain, heart, kidneys, and other organs, it revealed occipital brain function during the time she was beginning to see shadows and shapes, which was around 10 days before her transition home. This was clear evidence that the area of the brain responsible for vision was indeed functioning. For this scientist and physician, I am in awe with regard to the EEG and PET scan results, but my colleagues are not. Most found the results of the scan to be odd, especially in a blind woman with terminal cancer, but not improbable. They felt that the occipital cortex seemed to be similar to a patient with normal eyesight. However, her optic nerves were atrophied, signaling that there was no input from the retina to the visual cortex. They attributed the results to a metastatic cancerous lesion. As a scientist and physician, I understood where my colleagues were coming from, but, from a compassionate and God-loving man, I knew that the spheres of light, not picked up by the PET scan, were responsible for the results. As always, I will never cease to be amazed at the wondrous works of God.

4 The Exorcism of John L. Masters

And his fame went throughout all Syria: and they brought unto him all sick people that were taken with diseases and torments, and those which were possessed with devils, and those which were lunatic, and those that had the palsy; and he healed them.

—Matthew 4:24

In my 17 years as a physician, during which time I cared for thousands of terminally ill patients, I had never entertained the notion of evil spirits surrounding my gravely ill schizophrenic patients, let alone ascribing to the belief that they were possessed by a malevolent force. I did, however, have a handful of mentally competent patients who believed they had been visited by dark, impious angels, as well as bright, loving, and benevolent angels. On interviewing these patients about their sinister spiritual experiences, they often spoke of a dreadful and spine-chilling coldness that would settle in the room during their appearance. I always listened to my patients intently and with compassion, but at the end of the day I found a scientific reason for these occurrences, and almost always attributed them to unresolved physical, emotional, social, and spiritual issues that were being projected by the subconscious mind. It was in this manner that I could pinpoint the problems and then determine how to attain resolution or closure, before their death. In their defense, I do have to say that, on several occasions, I do recall feeling an unnatural and unnerving feeling as I entered the rooms of these patients alongside several of the nurses on the hospice unit. In fact, it was the nurses who were more intimately acquainted with these frightful happenings. One specific story I recall the nurses mentioning was about the chilling account of room 315.

One evening, during the midnight-to-morning shift, a nurse and a nurse's aid entered room 315 to bathe the patient. Just before they entered the room, they both felt a wave of extremely cold air circulate from the bottom of the door. Expecting to feel the coldness pour from the room, they went back and put on their sweaters. (Anyone who has ever worked or slept alongside an ill family member in a hospital during the late shift surely understands the need for sweaters.) As they opened the door, they were immediately struck by the drastic change in temperature. The room was warm, and the patient was seemingly comfortable. After they finished bathing the teenage girl, they quietly walked toward the beautifully stained, 9-foot-tall, solid wooden door.

Just prior to exiting the room, the nurses felt a similar wave of coldness, but this time coming from the rear. The draft differed this time, in that it was more forceful and sinister. This stream of frigid air seemed to navigate through their torsos, and, in what appeared to be one or two seconds, it immediately dissipated. Despite the haunting feeling that surrounded them for the rest of the evening, they discounted the incident as related to the natural flow of air. They said the scientific explanation was almost always easier to digest. It was not until the death of the patient in room 315 that more stories began to surface. From moving objects to extremely cold air in the room while the heater was on, and dark shadows seen entering the room, the stories were numerous and beyond comprehension. Was this a result of the 18-year-old schizophrenic woman, the room itself, or something different? The closest I got to an explanation was when the patient's mother told me that the girl's deceased father would dabble in dark magic, attempting to invoke the force of darkness to heal his daughter. Having been a witness to the power of his magic, the little girl's mother felt the haunting events, both at home and in the hospital, were being spun by here dead husband. "I believe he was still trying to heal our daughter, but from the dark side. This was sad, because my husband's actions convicted him for what I felt to be an eternal separation from God."

I told her I did not believe this form of reasoning, because thousands of my patients, some of whom also dabbled in the occult, relayed the love and forgiveness that awaits us all as we transition from this world to the next. The only willed thought that would keep one separated from our loving Creator was self-indictment. Yet, this method of self-sentencing our awareness to enter a dormant state was never permanent. The great news was that God would never leave our sides, no matter how cold and dark our souls were, as he created all souls and all souls were made in his likeness or essence. In this way, he would always live within every entity, where he would never cease from rekindling our awareness of the greater good within. If no unconditional loving parent could condemn his children to an eternal life of pain, then how could God, who loves us infinitely more, ever abandon us?

God has a way to deal with the suffering we invoked on others, but it is not by condemning his creation to eternal darkness. This next story is about the soul's two extreme sides, the conscious and unconscious, and how God helps us reconcile their actions with awareness of his perfect plan.

John L. Masters

John L. Masters was a 47-year-old agnostic with terminal stage-four lung cancer, liver metastases, and schizophrenia. As his delusions and aggressive behavior worsened, which coincided with his disease progression, he was eventually moved to a locked-down psychiatric ward within the oncology hospital. When I met John, I immediately sensed something ominous emanating from his being, which was not immediately visible or understood, but, in the end, awareness of it would lead me into understanding the area of our mind and soul known for its ability to manipulate one's own energy, as well as others', in order to create a dark and malignant consciousness for the purpose of self-service. Was this the ego, or something called our "sinful state"?

As I walked through the dreary halls of the three-story psychiatric ward, I glanced through the thick Plexiglas windows of each room, looking in with sadness at all those mentally ill patients who were being kept locked in their rooms. For me, the career I chose would act as a brutal reminder of man's successes and failures with regard to science and humanity. I was now privy to observing evil and goodness on a day-to-day basis, but with an emphasis on evil, as I would look into the cold, black eyes of John "Legion" Masters.

"Who gave you your middle name?"

"It was given to me by the motorcycle gang I hung out with. You see, we were all family, and our father, or leader, renamed us, taught us discipline, respect, and gave us religion."

"What was the religion they introduced you to?"

"The religion of the dark force and satanic worshiping. When we were baptized, we had our new name tattooed across our chest. My new name was 'Legion,' which meant mass, band, or division."

Legion, as he wanted to be called, spent most of the years with this gang, drinking, smoking, and injecting drugs. This lifestyle took its toll on many of his bike family, and Legion was not spared. After his diagnosis with lung cancer, liver metastasis, and advanced hepatitis C, he was treated with chemotherapy and radiation, but his malnutritioned body and abnormal liver function tests forced the oncologists to stop treatment.

"Dr. Lerma, they are inside me. I let them in and now I can't get rid of them. Please believe me! Why doesn't anyone believe me?"

"Legion, I want to help you. Tell me who is inside you, and what do they want?"

It was clear to me that John was delusional, so I listened to him intently, in hopes of subduing his behavior by getting him to trust me. There was no reason for me to believe that what he was telling me was true. After all, he was a delusional schizophrenic, and I was a logical scientist. I am not sure what the latter meant any longer, especially after the countless spiritual experiences I had witnessed.

"Dr. Lerma, please get me a Catholic priest. I know I am possessed by demons."

"Okay, Legion. I will see if I can find one."

Because he was beginning to get combative, the nurse gave him his ordered thorazine injection. Soon after the medicine was given, John began to get sleepy, so I finished the interview and the security guard opened the door for me. I walked out and toward the nurses' station. I asked the staff if John had told them he was possessed. The nurses said yes, and explained that John's psychiatrist felt he was manifesting a rare form of multiple personality disorder (MPD) to cope with his dying process. I had recalled, during my psychiatric rotation in medical school, that we learned how strong our egos were and how they were clever, but unintelligent, self-defeating, self-serving, and fearful of their own demise. So, I guess it was possible that John Masters's newly diagnosed MPD was the ego's desperate attempt at creating different personalities that were not dying, so as to survive. John's need to rid himself of these entities was total irony.

His ego was doing what it needed to survive, and his higher awareness or consciousness was seeking the ego's defeat. This sounded so much like an inner battle between good versus evil that we had learned in Bible school. Because the psychiatrist was treating his MPD, I felt it would be prudent and helpful to alleviate John's concerns by having a priest or minister provide spiritual support. The nurse on duty called the hospital chaplain, who happened to be a Catholic priest by the name of Father Doherty, and asked him to pay a visit to a terminally ill patient on the psychiatric ward. Father Doherty arrived later that evening, just as I was leaving.

He and I began to discuss John's disease process, including his advanced cancer, schizophrenia, and newly diagnosed MPD. I also detailed his life story, his association with an occult group that named him Legion, and his connection to all dark and unwanted souls. I explained that his recent diagnosis of MPD seem to coincide with his complaint of being possessed and desire to speak to a priest.

I decided to stay and observe John's interaction with Father Doherty, as I had not been a witness to a true personality disorder throughout my career. The guard, Father Doherty, and I entered John's room, which was close to the nurses' station, and was being closely monitored by surveillance cameras installed in his room. We found him sitting on the floor in a lotus-type position. After introducing Father Doherty to him, he slowly stood up and motioned for us to sit on the bed with him. He whispered his first few sentences as if to guard from others hearing. "Father, they are inside me. I let them in and they will not leave now. I am too tired to fight them. I am not lying. Please help me. I don't want to die like this. I want to go to heaven."

Father Doherty comforted him with a hug and a prayer, which seemed to bring peace to John.

Father Doherty: "Who is inside you, John?"

"Some evil spirits that do not want my soul to go with the loving spirits. They want me to stay with them here on earth after I die."

Father Doherty: "Why do they want you to stay on earth?"

"Because they are afraid if I go with God's angels, I may draw them with me into the light, which they feel is where judgment occurs."

Father Doherty: "What have they done to be so afraid of entering God's kingdom?"

"They have hurt so many souls on Earth and are responsible for many others veering from the light."

Father Doherty: "Do they not believe in God's forgiveness and unconditional love?"

"No. But I want to believe, Father. The angels that have been coming to see me along with my deceased parents and friends are telling me that my time is coming to an end here on Earth and they want to bring closure to my soul. They have allowed me to see many things that I have done, and are simultaneously letting me experience God's undying love for all souls, including those who have chosen to roam the Earth for eternity. I was told I needed to use my free will and God's love to defeat the lost souls that have invaded my mind and soul. Because I willfully let them in, I need to willfully ask them to leave by the power received from accepting and inviting God into our soul and total essence."

Father Doherty: "Have you been able to do this?"

"I am trying, but it is a lot harder than it seems. I am so filled with guilt that every time I go to release them, they work on my guilt and tell me I am not worthy to receive such a loving God. They show me all the darkness I caused to so many and try to tell me that I will be judged harshly and without compassion. They would rather stay on Earth than take the chance of a worse punishment. It makes sense to me. When they leave my body as the angels and my family appear, it is at this time that I long to be with them and am remorseful for my sins. They cannot do it for me but another human can certainly guide me through the process. I have to find the power and will to defeat these self-defeating spirits. Do you believe me and will you help me?"

Father. Doherty: "Yes, I do, and I will help you."

"Thank you. Thank you so very much!"

Father Doherty went on to tell John that he needed to go back to the church and get some holy water and a book of prayers to assist him in removing the dark forces from his mind and body.

As Father Doherty and I walked out of the room, I asked him to tell me more about the Roman Catholic Church's stance on exorcism. "In 1999, Pope John Paul II reportedly mandated that all Dioceses needed to become familiar with the prayer to exorcise evil spirits and the dark forces of Satan. It was at this time I was chosen, along with several other hospital chaplains, to learn the rites of exorcism. To date, the church does not discuss this openly, however. There are only a handful of priests I have spoken with who have been witnesses to several classic exorcisms. A classic possession is where the person under the influence of the devil is known to speak several languages, including Latin and Aramaic (the original language of the Bible), and has physical strength disproportionate to a person's age or body. A good friend of mine, by the name of Father Gabriele Amorth, is the Vatican's top exorcist to date. He told me that he preformed several hundred exorcisms last year in Italy alone. Pope John Paul II was known to have personally exorcised a demon from a teenage girl who claimed to be possessed by Satan and other spirits."

He went on to describe the process as he remembered it: The first phase includes reciting the "Imploring Formula," in which the evils of Satan are spoken and God is entreated to free the possessed. The second phase calls for invoking the "Intense Formula," at which time Satan is ordered to leave the possessed. As we were leaving the psychiatric ward, we felt a rush of cold air come from behind us. The nurse, who was sitting at the nurses' station, looked at both of us with fear. "Did you feel that, Dr. Lerma?"

I nodded in affirmation as I reached up to check if air was blowing from the vents.

"Did you feel anything, Dr. Lerma?" Father Doherty asked.

"Nope," I remarked.

Father Doherty asked me if I wanted to come back in the morning to witness the prayers against Satan and his evil spirits. Quite curious as to what an exorcism was like, I agreed to join him. I reviewed what had transpired and asked John's only relative, and power of attorney, James, if Father Doherty could pray over John, as he had requested, to cleanse his soul and mind from his sinful past. James replied, "It's about time someone cared enough to help my brother. I told so many doctors in the past that my brother was dabbling in the occult and his mental changes were likely from evil possession. Thank you, Father Doherty and Dr. Lerma. I will pray for his soul's purification."

When I arrived home later that evening, the nurse caring for John called to let me know that he had just awoke from his sleep screaming and bouncing on the bed uncontrollably. The nurse reported that he was awake during the episode, which had now subsided, and had no past history of seizures. I ordered to hold the thorazine, as this might be causing his seizures, and ordered lorazepam to calm his nerves. I also asked the nurse to get an electroencephalogram (EEG) as well as an MRI of his head. I wanted to rule out seizures and brain metastasis. When I arrived the next morning to make rounds at the psychiatric ward, I saw Father Doherty speaking to the nurse from the night shift. They were reviewing the videotape that showed John's entire body bouncing on his bed as he yelled out undecipherable words. The EEG was negative for a seizure, and his MRI was essentially normal. It was possible that the EEG may not have picked up a seizure, so I empirically started him on phenytoin, which was an anti-seizure medication.

The nurse went on to tell us that, besides John's possible seizures, they were frightened by the eerie scratches and clawing coming from the walls in John's room, as well as waves of cold air. One nurse stated, "It was like the things that happened to that little girl in the movie *The Exorcist*."

Father Doherty and I proceeded to examine and talk to John. What I found anomalous after examining John were his mental alertness and strength. You see, most people who suffer from a seizure or major psychotic break would be very lethargic, sluggish, and drowsy for at least 24 hours after the cerebral event. Now add the fact that John was terminally ill, weighing less than 100 pounds, severely cachectic, and having visions of angels and deceased loved ones. I knew this meant one thing for John and countless other terminally ill patients with a sudden resurgence of energy: The soul was preparing to be guided by the angels back home. Father Doherty looked at me and said, "Dr. Lerma, it appears as though we have been given a sign that our time is limited with what we must do." At that moment, John forcefully said, "I am ready to confront my demons and move forward with the angels.

"John, are the angels here?"

"Absolutely."

"How many are there, and what do they look like?"

"There must be 50 to 60, not including my friends and parents. They are singing a beautiful song to God, Dr. Lerma. I have never heard it, but it's making me feel so joyous, peaceful, and totally loved. The angels I am seeing are not the same ones that have been coming to me for the last two to three weeks. These are much bigger and much brighter. I can see their golden hair, deep blue and brown eyes, and flowing deep maroon to white robes."

"Where are they, and are they speaking to you?"

"They are on both sides of my bed, and above and below as well. It is as though there are no walls, no ceiling or floor. We must be floating. Wow! One of the biggest angels, with wings more than 20 feet long and feathers whiter than snow, is full of light and love, and wants me to know that my will to be with God has healed me so I can fight the Prince of Darkness. Dr. Lerma, that is why I am full of energy. I believe all your patients that have this surge of energy are also healed just before being taken back home. I can see the tunnel of light in the distance. It is calling out to me, Dr. Lerma. It is so loving and forgiving. It wants to teach me more about love and forgiveness so I can help many more that are to follow."

At that moment, Father Doherty and I felt a warm, embracing hug, but no one was around us. Father Doherty said to welcome it, as it was the powerful love and grace of God that had penetrated our entire body.

Father Doherty began with a prayer, followed by sprinkling of holy water on John, the nurse, the entire room, and me. He then began reciting the imploring formula followed by the imperative formula. Father Doherty was now placing his hands on John as he asked the evil ones to depart from his body. At that moment, John's face turned pale, then red, and his upper body and extremities began to shake. After a few seconds the shaking stopped and his face turned pale once more. He told us he could feel the spirits surfacing and was fighting them. He fell asleep for several minutes, and, when he woke up, he was screaming obscenities and phrases that did not make sense. Father Doherty said he heard a few Latin words mixed with unintelligible words. Two of the words he heard were *Satan* and *Legion*.

So Father Doherty began denouncing Satan and ordering him to leave John's body and soul. "Legion, creature of God, in the name of God who created you and Jesus Christ who died for you, I require you to hear my voice as the voice of Christ's Church, and although I am but a humble and unworthy servant, obey my commands."

The glass of water, the Kleenex box, and the pitcher of water all flew off the end table clearly and landed almost 4 feet away. Was this possible? Did those objects fly off the table by themselves? The table was at least 6 feet from John and the rest of us. If it was the spirits, then how could they manipulate atoms from another dimension? The energy needed to move the objects must have been immense. I then thought about telekinesis and ESP. I thought, if these psychic abilities existed in humans, then it was possible that John moved them by the projection of thought or psychokinesis. I had heard about experiments in Russia, Japan, and here in the United States, where people with extrasensory and extra kinetic abilities were being studied. If these abilities existed in humans, then a part of John's brain, in response to his psychotic break, could unknowingly be creating the entire possession phenomena. This was not only possible, but also probable.

How could I explain the shadows and images on the TV monitor and the extreme temperature changes associated with John's possession? Was it possible that John was projecting mental images into the camera, the film, and our minds? This thought really frightened me, as the implications were far-reaching. I could see why the governments of Russia, Japan, and the United States were interested in this phenomenon.

I then heard John exclaim, "It's Archangel Michael. He is the angel I described earlier. He is directing the band of evil spirits away from me and toward the light. Michael is telling the lost souls that God wants to help and not condemn them. All they have to do is trust, accept, and enter the Light of non-judgment, non-condemnation, and total love. Father Doherty, I wish you could see the souls you helped drive out of my mind and body."

With tears in his eyes, John Masters positioned his body on his bed and looked straight up at the ceiling, sighed, and closed his eyes. With his eyes still closed, he gently said that the lost souls were now slowly moving toward the light of God amongst an assembly of angels. This is what it was all about. I now see clearly. I see I had chosen to play a role as John L. Masters so that I could draw a group of God's lost souls into me and eventually out of me and toward the light. Wow! I am awe-struck at the extent God goes to bring one or more sheep back to his flock.

I could almost picture what John was seeing. It was certainly beautiful. John fell asleep minutes later, and Father Doherty and I went home feeling physically exhausted, but with a sense of love and peace I had never felt. John was called later that evening to go back home. I pictured Archangel Michael flying through the tunnel, carrying John on his brilliantly white and soft-feathered wings, and feeling nothing but peace and love. My mind and soul were now filled with knowledge to explain this supernatural event, but this knowledge was not one I could write down on paper or vocalize to others. It was the knowledge that words were spoken through acts of compassion, empathy, kindness, forgiveness, and, above all, unconditional love.

Doctor's Notes and More Conversations With John and Father Doherty

...The gate to the carnal self is four-fold: sight, sound, taste, and touch. A demon can come in through any of the five gates by tempting the guard at the door. If the guard allows the demon in, then the demon has authority to move about freely. You gave him this authority by giving up your free-will to stand and rebuke the temptation.

—Chris Ward

A few weeks after John's death, I went back to the psychiatric unit to review the video to carefully document the unusual events that occurred throughout John's three-week stay. Unfortunately, more than 80 percent of the video was lost or damaged. However, the remaining parts were astounding. At 1 a.m., I noticed on the video that there was a blanket of darkness hovering over John while he slept. It hovered in the room like smoke, and then disappeared as it settled over John. At 2 a.m., John awoke and began to shake, and, while lying in a horizontal position, his entire body went airborne, almost 2 feet in the air. John was awake during this event as he was shouting, "Help me." After 20 seconds, John's body stopped bouncing on the bed. The video goes blank. I fast-forwarded ahead almost two hours, at which point I saw John sitting on the side of his bed, looking up at the corner of the room, and talking. The odd thing was that you could not hear him utter a single word. The tape was picking up background noise, including the sound of John moving about, so either John was just mouthing his words or he was not emitting any vocal tones, similar to how many other patients had acted when they were talking to the angels. Of interest was the area of the room John was looking at and speaking to. Again, countless other patients had reported seeing the angels come forth from the corners and leave through the upper corners of the room.

To this day I cannot come up with a decent hypothesis to explain why three-dimensional corners are nests for spirits. Is that part of the reason the Egyptians built the pyramids, which had three perfect corners? Could it be that the pharaohs learned about spirits and corners, and wanted to create them perfectly for spirit corners from the afterlife to return through? Their deep desire to learn about life after death inspired them to write the *Egyptian Book of the Dead*. Several hours later, I saw John lying on his bed looking at the end table, almost 6 feet from his bed.

Within minutes, I noticed that the pitcher of water began to shake and subsequently fell forward, spilling the water. This portion of the video offers some credence to psychokinesis. I did notice a small but brilliant white light emanating from the forward right corner of the room in relation to his bed. It slowly grew to the size of a basketball before it contracted back to a barely noticeable light. I was curious to see if there was any marking left in that corner, which happened to be the same corner John was speaking toward, so I went to the unoccupied room and turned on the lights. I went to the corner in question, and, almost

8 feet up, I found a circular imprinted image, almost the size of a basketball, at the area I had seen the light. It was not a burn mark, marker, or dust, as it would not wash off. None of the other corners exhibited any thing remotely similar.

I was hoping that the last day of video, when Father Doherty was attempting an exorcism on John Masters, had not been damaged or erased. When I reached the day and hour, I noticed that the initial images were obscured by static. What I saw and heard next was beyond explanation. I saw Father Doherty praying over John while I was looking at John. It was then that the objects on the end table were thrown outward by a seemingly unseen force. The box of Kleenex, glass, and pitcher of water all flew 4 to 5 feet from the table. A smoke-like entity was now coming from the left corner of the room, opposite the corner with the bright light, and slowly moved toward John. I could now see it enter John's body through the top of his head; simultaneously, John's body went into what appeared to be controlled seizures. Within minutes of this event, a dark essence left John's body from his head again, and John began to smile. He looked up at Father Doherty and me, then looked directly upward and began to talk to Archangel Michael. I could hear John thanking Michael and telling him to take care of his friends who were also lost.

A few hours later, around the time of John's death, I know I saw the most beautiful white light shoot out of his solar plexus region toward the right corner of the room. I knew that there was no way to explain this to my colleagues, but, then again, why did I need to explain? What this beautiful experience left me with was a reason to continue practicing my passion: to serve my fellow man and terminally ill patients with compassion, kindness, and, above all, unconditional love.

Exorcism Facts

The following is what Father Doherty taught me about church and possession.

First, remember that genuine possessions are a very rare phenomenon, but real. The diagnosis, similar to evil, is not one to be bandied about. Christianity has historically taught that Satan and his legion of demons roam about the world seeking energy by instilling fear into humans. Christian, Muslim, and Jewish scriptures detail the belief that evil spirits can come to possess a mind and body, resulting in unnatural behavior. It is known now that many of the people in the past, who were thought to be possessed by a demon, were actually suffering from physical ailments such as seizures and schizophrenia. A significant part of the Gospel message relates to Jesus's healing ministry of exorcism.

The Vatican states that Jesus cured sick people by casting out one or more demons from their bodies. Jesus preformed an exorcism where he commanded the evil spirits from a person to move to a herd of pigs. Another scripture that speaks about possession and exorcism is Matthew 10:1. "And when he had called unto him his 12 disciples, he gave them power against unclean spirits, to cast them out, and to heal all manner of sickness and all manner of disease."

5 A Night Mapped Out by Providence

Having worked 24-hour shifts the previous four weeks, and averaging 15 to 20 hours a day in the hospital, I seriously considered little Sarah's advice to go out to a nice restaurant for a relaxing and healthy dinner. "Dr. Lerma, you are telling *me* I should eat? Well, you need to eat, because your pants are going to fall off one day, and that will be too funny."

I laughed and then cried, as I reflected about what this beautifully graceful and selfless 12-year-old girl with terminal cancer was conveying. My heart was so battered by the thought of losing one of the most self-sacrificing, self-denying, and altruistic people I knew in this world.

I remembered the words Sarah's mother spoke after the diagnosis. "God, why Sarah? Why my little baby? She has always been a caring daughter, sister, and friend to many. It's not fair. It is just not fair. Please, my Lord, help my little girl."

Who was I to tell a loving mother that her daughter had no chance of survival and that the treatment for her cancer had failed? No matter the number of patients I had comforted before their death, no matter how many angelic stories I was told, or how many mystical experiences I had witnessed, telling a parent that his or her child was terminally ill was unnatural and exceedingly heart-wrenching. In medical school, we were taught to keep our fellow man from dying, not to let them die. Incredibly, the irony was so thick you could cut it with a knife. The words *why Sarah* kept echoing through my head.

At some point, I was comforted by my past patients as they reminded me of the hopeful and reassuring stories they had left me. I now clearly remembered their beautiful messages and revelations of an all-loving, all-forgiving, and non-condemning Creator. I wanted so much to have Sarah's mother sense and be conscious of the comforting and miraculous hand of God and his angels, as I had experienced throughout the years as a hospice physician. The best I could do was to care for her daughter as if she were my own, and in time to convey the loving, hopeful, and uplifting stories given to me for this very purpose.

As I walked toward my car, the cool breeze from the Gulf of Mexico gently converged with my somber face and seemed to wake me from my slump. It was rather magical, but the October breezes in Texas were known to be alluring. As fate would have it, my sudden spiritedness and ebullience reminded me of Sarah's caring and protective persona. I wondered for a moment if the enchanting fall breeze was Sarah's soul luring me away from the hospice unit and toward my favorite sushi restaurant in down-town Houston. Just like that, I found myself in my technologically advanced car with rich Corinthian leather seats. Yes, a Yugo. I was doing my part to help our planet.

I was intoxicated by the evening's beauty and I felt that the rest of the evening was mapped out by divine providence. From a distance, the sight of the shimmering lights from the glass-covered skyscrapers was breathtaking. Houston's downtown skyline was one of the best in the world.

As I arrived at the restaurant, I entered Zaki's parking lot, and for some unclear reason I chose a space furthest away from the restaurant and closest to the street. When I turned off the car, I noticed two children, around 10 and 15 years old, and their father standing at the corner of the street waiting for the city bus. They were giddy and joyful, much like Sarah. They saw my little car and smiled. They probably thought it was a toy car, and wondered what a grown man was doing riding in it. I smiled and waved, as the children skipped toward the convenience store, where I am sure candy was the food of choice. The father also waved back and watched intently to make sure his little girls were safe. It was inconceivable how this one family was in total bliss while only a few miles away, another family's life had been turned upside down.

As I began to contemplate Sarah, my cell phone's ring startled me. It was Mary, the nurse caring for Sarah. She was calling to ask advice about Sarah's change in consciousness. After falling asleep, her respiratory rate began to drop, as well as her temperature, pulse, blood pressure, and urine output. Despite these changes, Sarah remained quite peaceful, without any signs of distress, including pain, anxiety, and dyspnea. Sarah had not received any sedatives or opiates in the prior eight hours, so I knew this was related to her disease advancing. I told Mary I was coming back, but she urged me to at least eat before I returned, as Sarah was very comfortable and sleeping soundly. I hesitated for a moment, at which point Mary replied, "Dr. Lerma, Sarah made it clear to all the nurses on the unit that she was worried about you and wanted all of us in the hospice wing to make sure you ate and rested. After all, Dr. Lerma, do not forget that most patients need some uninterrupted time to converse with their angels before they transition."

I reluctantly agreed and told the nurse I would be back as soon as I ate, but I asked the nurse to place the phone to Sarah's ear so I might comfort her. Mary walked into Sarah's room and placed the portable phone to her right ear. "*It's Dr. Lerma. I am out eating like you said, and I wanted to tell you how great of a friend you are and how much I love you. If you need to go before I get back, I understand fully. I want you to be at peace and enjoy flying next to God's angels and dolphins. Have loads of fun. You deserve the treasures God is about to give you. Pray for all of us that remain here on Earth and know that I will always love you.*"

Was it possible that Sarah knew she was going to pass that night, and waited for me to leave? I knew more than 70 to 80 percent of all patients would wait to transition from this world to the next when all the people they were emotionally tied to would step away from the room. When this did not occur, patients having pre-death experiences told me that many souls could linger in our world in spiritual distress. They explained that their spiritual distress was out of concern for the loved one(s) who did not get or give closure. I do believe it is crucial for everyone emotionally connected to the patient to spend one-on-one time with them, at which point they resolve issues and get reassurance that their surviving family members would be cared for, especially their spouse and children.

Amazingly, I have witnessed hundreds of families who have flat out refused to give their ill loved ones the needed closure and mutual forgiveness to transition from this world to he next in a peaceful manner. These patients usually die with significant social, emotional, and spiritual pain. The types of disquieting pain experienced by all humans include physical, emotional, interpersonal pain, and existential pain. Parents with terminally ill children need to give closure as well, but many children will wait for one or both parents to be close to them so their child is comforted in knowing that their parents and siblings can eventually lead a loving, joyful, and productive life. With closure given and obtained, the child's soul can be guided to God's Heavenly Kingdom by the love of their parents and siblings, along with the angels and loved ones who have passed on.

I stepped out of my car and headed for the restaurant. Within seconds of finishing my telephone conversation, I heard a horrific crashing sound and saw a four-door SUV literally hurdling through the air and heading toward me as I stood outside my car. I attempted to escape its trajectory by running, but the speed with which it was heading toward me forced me to change my plan of escape. It was now clear that there was no escaping the metallic debris, fuel, and finely sharpened pieces of glass that spewed from the car. My mind and body went into self-preservation mode and began to dissect the entire scene, frame by frame, in order to determine the best plan for survival. The only option left was to squat and use my hands to cover my head. I do not recall seeing angels or my life pass before my eyes, but I definitely recall that every cell of my being was permeated by heavenly peace. Could this peace be emanating from the angels encircling this horrifying tragedy?

The next thing I remember was the sound of the SUV coming to a screeching halt as it crashed into a 5-foot metal guard firmly bolted onto the outer edge of the parking lot. Airborne pieces of metal, broken glass, and oil ended their momentum as they struck my body and the hood of my car. I looked up and saw the car only 10 feet from me. It was by the grace of God, and I am sure with Sarah's protection, that the metal guards surrounding the parking lot saved my life. The feelings of serenity and peace, as well as the changes of time and space, dissipated rapidly as if to make room for new emotions of utter disbelief, shock, and a new sense of reality. Everything around me was now moving at its normal pace. As I stood up and looked around, all I could see was a thick cloud of dark-gray to black smoke covering the entire crash scene. I immediately called 911 from my cell phone and alerted them to an accident with possible fatalities. As the dust and smoke began to settle, the previously indistinct sounds of anguish began to pervade the entire area. I heard the most frightening and unnatural sounds of deep sobbing moans. As the smoke had not cleared, I found it exceedingly difficult to locate where the sounds were originating from, so I walked around the crash scene, and quickly triaged the injured. Two victims were still sitting in their car, awake and moving, but in shock. Two others in separate cars were unresponsive with critical scalp and facial injuries. I instructed some of the bystanders on how to stabilize their necks and minimize bleeding by direct pressure. I heard someone shout out that there was a man and a woman badly injured.

As I approached the flipped vehicle, I noticed that it was the SUV that nearly struck me, but it was mangled beyond recognition. The man and woman in the front seat were conscious but in shock. There was a copious amount of smoke coming from the engine and with the smell of gasoline, I feared that the car would catch fire. With help from one of the waiters from the Japanese restaurant, we managed to get the woman out of the vehicle, and placed her a safe distance from the car. We went back to get the gentleman, but soon realized there was no possible way to remove him from harm's way, as his waist and lower extremities were pinned under the car. As I lay on the cement, I could see through a wedge made by the roof of the car, the curb, and the street that his legs were crushed and bleeding profusely. With the sound of the emergency vehicles approaching, I noticed a large amount of blood around his neck. In an attempt to locate the bleeding so as to apply pressure, I removed the wires and bent metal from around his throat.

As I applied pressure with my shirt, the man said, "Thank you. My name is Daniel. What's yours?"

"My name is Johnnie, and I am a physician who is here to help you. Please keep talking to me and don't fall asleep. The fire department is here and we will have you out of this car in an instant."

I yelled out to the paramedics that we needed to lift this car immediately. I turned back to face Daniel and asked if he was in pain, but he said no. *"Well, that's good. Remember Daniel: God loves you and is here with you, along with his angels."*

"Doctor, you are the man that waved to me from your car," Daniel replied.

My heart sank at the frightening realization that Daniel was the man I saw standing with his children only a few feet away from me. The entire scope of the accident struck deep in my heart and soul.

"This could have been me," I thought to myself.

I asked Daniel, almost in a panic, where the children who were standing next to him were. His answer painted even a more chilling picture in my mind. "There were no children next to me, Doctor."

"But Daniel, when you thought I was waving at you, I was actually waving back to the children next to you."

"I was standing alone, Doctor, and I have no children," Daniel replied. As I thought Daniel's memory was affected by his critical injuries, I apprised the paramedics that there maybe two children, around the ages of 10 to 15, unaccounted for.

As I heard the paramedics helping the injured, and the firemen getting the tools to lift the car, I caressed Daniel's head, and prayed the Our Father. Daniel said that was his favorite prayer, and so he joined in. "Doctor," Daniel replied with a now faint voice. "Don't worry about the children or me. I think you may have mistaken the angels around us for the children."

This was the first time I had an accident victim relay a possible angelic vision. Was Daniel having a pre-death vision, similar to the ones terminally ill patients spoke of before transitioning? Daniel fit this terminal situation in light of the amount of blood loss he had suffered. At this point it was not up to me to question the validity of the apparitions. Rather, it was up to me to comfort this critically injured gentleman until the paramedics and firemen were able extract him without further injury. In an attempt to keep Daniel awake, I engaged him in conversation about the angels. I asked him to describe the angels and how they made him feel. "Doctor, do you believe in God and his angels?" Daniel asked.

"Of course I do. In fact, many of my patients have shared their beautiful experiences regarding these loving entities."

Daniel replied, "I'm glad you do. You know, they are real. I thought I was seeing things that should not be there, but I was told they were real and here to make me feel good. I think they want me to follow them. I want to go with them. The angels are so loving and beautiful. Some even look like children. They have made me feel so peaceful, and I am not scared at all now."

"What are the angels doing, Daniel?"

Daniel replied, "It looks like two are holding the car up so it doesn't cave in on my whole body. There is also one standing next to you and it's a little girl holding on to your coat. I think it's your little girl, Doctor. She is so beautiful."

I looked next to me but did not see the angels or the little girl. *"That is not my girl, Daniel."*

Daniel replied, "Well she is standing right next to you and is still holding on to your coat."

I was almost sure Daniel was delirious and hallucinating, and these visions were the brain's way of comforting him. Still, I continued the conversation, as it seemed to make him comfortable. *"What is her name, Daniel?"*

Daniel hesitated for a moment and then said the word *Sarah*. When I heard that name, my eyes must have popped out of my head. Daniel went on to tell me that she was a very loving girl and that she was next to me because I had helped her feel better before she died. "Doctor, do you know this girl named Sarah, and was she a patient of yours?" Daniel asked.

"Daniel, the only patient I have had named Sarah, is a patient I currently have in the hospital. In fact, she was the one who suggested that I go out to eat and relax, as I had been on call for the last 36 hours."

Daniel answered, "This is your patient. She is here now."

My heart fluttered with the proposition that Sarah's spirit was standing next to me. I was in total awe and had goose bumps. I slowly looked downward and to my right, hoping in some way to see the little girl, but of course I didn't. If Sarah had passed, like Daniel said, then I would have received a call from the nurse alerting me to that fact. But how did he know her name? Had I mentioned it without knowing? Did Daniel have a form of telepathy, which several prominent medical scientists believed could be present during stressful situations? Was Daniel having hallucinations and illusions related to this trauma? I then heard the paramedic tell me to move, as they were about to lift the car with a winch. I told Daniel we were going to lift the car so we could pull him out.

In a cryptic response, Daniel smiled and said, "I am finally going to be healed forever. Don't worry about me, Dr. Lerma."

As I stood back from the car, my phone rang. It was the hospital. "Dr. Lerma, I am so sorry to tell you this, but Sarah just passed away." I nearly dropped the phone, as I grew weak and pale. I could hear Mary asking if I was okay several times. I reluctantly placed the phone to my ear and told her I was taken aback, but fine. *"What happened, Mary? She was speaking to me a short while ago."*

Mary went on to explain that she began to decline after I left, and then proceeded to wait for her mother to step out for coffee. When the aid and Mary went in to change her sheets she looked at them with a big smile and said she was tired. She closed her eyes and in a matter of seconds the room felt energized with static energy, which dissipated shortly afterward. As they looked down toward Sarah, she was still smiling, but her spirit was no longer in her worn-out body.

By this time Mary was overwhelmed with so much emotion that I began to cry and shake from sadness and disbelief. *"Mary, I just witnessed an accident where a critically ill gentleman, who is still pinned under a car, told me he saw a little girl next to me by the name of Sarah. There was no girl beside me. He told me she was a patient of mine who I had comforted before she died. I thought he was delirious until you just called and told me she had passed."*

I composed myself and told Mary I would call her back, because I needed to go back and help Daniel. The car was now off his legs, and the paramedics placed tourniquets at proximal regions in an attempt to decrease the blood loss. They also started intravenous fluids on both arms so as to increase blood volume and the overall blood pressure. As they worked on Daniel, I noticed that he was less alert, but I knew he could hear me, like almost all my patients could before they died.

I knelt down next to the gurney and whispered into his ear, "*Daniel, it's Doctor Johnnie. You are right; Sarah is next to me. Please tell her I love her as I love you, my friend.*" Amazingly, Daniel whispered into my ear that Sarah was waiting for him to go into the light. He pointed to an area above the wrecked SUV and said, "The light is so beautiful. I am so...."

The paramedics heard Daniel mention the light, and they checked his pulse and rhythm, only to find out that he was in ventricular fibrillation. They immediately started CPR and placed him in the ambulance. I held his hand as they placed him in the ambulance, and told him to pray for all of us in this tough world. As I saw the ambulance pull away, I was almost certain that I saw Daniel sitting up alongside Sarah and waving goodbye.

I stood contemplating what had happened that evening. I was used to helping people who were terminally ill transition to a peaceful and loving realm, but this was beyond what I could ever imagine doing. Because Sarah and I had grown very fond of each other, was it possible that I sensed her need to be alone before she passed, and negotiated to journey further than my apartment, across the street from the hospital? If this was true, then why did I witness such a horrific accident? Everything occurred as though I was in the wrong place at the wrong time. Yet, how could I believe I was in the wrong place at the wrong time, when in actuality, I was witness to one of the most astonishing and awe-inspiring events in my life? If this were true, then I must have been at the right place at the right time.

As Sarah told me once, "We cannot escape suffering in this world, even if you try. Suffering is not just cancer or accidents; it is just living in a world where darkness and goodness live. We should always want to be close to God, because he will always save us. So, suffering is only bad if you see it that way. If you see it as good and give it back to God, then you will see the infinite blessings and rewards it will bring to you and the world. I know it's difficult to understand this, but know it is true."

This gentleman, who I only knew for less than 30 minutes, left me with such a feeling of hope and love in the midst of a dreadful and daunting tragedy. I guess Sarah was right when she said that other people's suffering, if given up to God, can affect scores of souls around the world in a positive and hopeful way.

Doctor's Notes

A few days after the accident, I attended my clinic. My first patient was Mrs. Lopez. In a series of events that were more than mere coincidences, Mrs. Lopez told me she rescheduled her visit from Tuesday, the day of the accident, to Friday, as her daughter was in town and wanted to visit with me. I placed Mrs. Lopez and her daughter in the same room, and somehow the conversation turned to a fatal car accident her daughter's best friend, J.R., was involved in a few days prior. She said he had killed a man by trapping him under a truck. I couldn't believe what I was hearing. In a city of more than 5 million people, here was a lady who knew the man who was the cause of the tragedy. I was so upset.

She went on to tell me that he was drunk, and that evening in jail, he told Mrs. Lopez's daughter that he had a vision of the man who died, along with a little girl. J.R. was so remorseful, and promised to change his life. He served two years in prison for manslaughter, where he continued to have almost weekly visions of Daniel and Sarah. He went on to college and received his psychology degree, which he uses to help schoolchildren with drug and alcohol problems. He also works closely with Mothers Against Drunk Divers (MADD), as well as churches and synagogues, where he gives talks about his life as a drug and alcohol abuser, and how those bad decisions led him to kill a young man in a car accident, who he believed suffered selflessly to save his soul. He discusses the visions of Daniel and a little girl named Sarah, and the messages he has received from them regarding suffering, forgiveness, hope, and love. He has personally gone to ask for forgiveness from Daniel's family, and now Daniel's mother and J.R. go to church together.

Was it possible that Daniel chose to help save J.R.'s soul? If so, did this mean we plan our lives before being born into this world? Does God help us construct our earthly lives?

I do recall patients of mine voicing a common angelic message regarding free will and its existence before taking our first breath in this world. All souls that desire to enter the human body do so with a loving enthusiasm to bring about heaven on Earth by using their gift of free will to invoke God within themselves. In other words, I am told that souls choose to be born on Earth, so they can fully comprehend the power of free will and exercise that power to reconcile darkness and goodness, or ego and higher self to become one with God.

When those two are gathered or reconciled with self-love and self-forgiveness via free will, the ultimate higher self, or God, is born into our awareness. This unselfish choice to invite God into our lives allows one to create heaven on Earth. With the powers of God within, miracles will be carried out in the name of Jesus. Unfortunately, most mentally and physically capable people choose to reconcile their two sides on their deathbed. Although it is still a great accomplishment, not doing it sooner in life robs the soul of experiencing "the one thing" they were destined to do on Earth through the invitation of God within our souls. Having realized "the one thing" would have automatically given one an eternal wealth of unconditional love for their self and others, including memories of helping others and creating miracles through the God within. In essence, those who listen to the voice within—that is, the Holy Spirit—will surely come to experience their divine destiny at a time in their lives that will assure a fulfilling and meaningful life and death. Waiting to understand and visualize how one's life would have played out, had they had faith to pursue, will usually allow the power of guilt to consume them. The good news, I am told, is that God understands the grueling challenges we all face in this world, and as such will never stop helping us learn how to utilize his greatest gift to us: free will. To help us through these arduous, guilt-ridden times, God sends us a multitude of angels and loved ones to assist us in finding self-love and self-forgiveness, allowing one to finally accept and believe in God's unconditional forgiveness.

If people are terminally ill and having a difficult time forgiving themselves for whatever they did or did not do, angels will usually begin to appear around four weeks before their transition. Some may have angels as early as four to six months before their death. It all depends on the amount of time needed to help the patient understand and accept that God loves them and has already forgiven them. One would think if one saw angels or God, they would automatically be remorseful and reconcile, so they could move forward to the loving and joyful light. IOn the contrary, a few individuals have had such entrenched guilt that they cannot find it within themselves to accept God's forgiveness. Many patients have told me that, although one may pass with guilt, God and his angels have ways of helping those souls on the other side to finally accept his love and forgiveness.

Psalm 139 talks about God's unconditional love for King David, who was filled with guilt, by telling him he will always be with him, even in heaven or hell. Still, it has to be horrible to die with guilt. Other patients who do not want to die with guilt choose to use their free will to prolong the suffering on their deathbed, as they believe this will alleviate the guilt and self-conviction enough to allow their souls to accept God's love and forgiveness.

I have learned from my loving patients that it is not difficult to lead a peaceful and fruitful life. One has to listen to his heart, and use his free will located in his solar plexus to yearn for a better life, goodness, self-love, forgiveness, and God. In this manner, God will set one's life path through grace.

With regard to the planning of our lives before our birth, Sarah told me that some souls are too overzealous to make a difference and choose extremely demanding and punishing lives. However, God is intimately involved in the architecture of our earthly role, and assures he will never allow a soul to engage in a role that is beyond their capacity to endure.

J.R. told me that in a recent vision, Daniel spoke of "the one thing," and how the meaning behind these words was the key to a fulfilling life on earth and heaven. Apparently, J.R. said that Daniel would not elaborate on it further except that the meaning of "the one thing" was within and different for each soul. J.R. felt that God had placed the complete understanding of this concept within all of us. All we had to do was pray, meditate, and listen to God. I agreed with Daniel that the knowledge of "the one thing" of which he so cryptically spoke is different for everyone. When I asked my 16-year-old son, Mark, what he felt God meant by the statement, he replied, "That's easy, Dad. It's our individualistic God-given passion. It is that one desire God placed in all our hearts to pursue through faith, self-love, and self-forgiveness, so that our lives would be fulfilling, joyful, meaningful, and, above all, one with God." I was taken aback by Mark's response, as it was so profound and right on the money. My son went on to divulge that his passion centered around helping people who were ill, with the priority being God first, then his family.

Roswell

...Roswell was a real incident, and that indeed an alien craft did crash, and that material was recovered from that crash site. We all know UFOs are real. All we need to ask is where are they from.

—Astronaut Dr. Edgar Mitchell, 1971

Colonel Marshall Bradfield first explained NASA's and Jet Propulsion Laboratory's (JPL) cover mission to search for intelligent life in space. On August 20, 1977, and September 5, 1977, two spacecrafts were launched from the Kennedy Space Flight Center in Florida. They were called Voyager I and II, and each one carried a message. On a gold-plated record, Bach's *Brandenburg Concerto #2* was unanimously chosen to be the first sound that our extraterrestrial brothers and sisters would hear. It was chosen because it most accurately captured the essence of peace and beauty of our planet and the human race. With the beautiful sound of violins, trumpets, and flutes playing the spoken words from a gentle and sophisticated gentleman read,

"I send greetings on behalf of the people of our planet. We step out of our solar system into the universe, seeking only peace...."

Men, women, and children recorded greetings in all the engaging languages of the world. This gold-plated record depicting images, music, and sounds of our planet was arranged in a manner that had the highest probability of being understood, if ever intercepted by an unearthly and technologically advanced civilization.

Thirteen years after its launch, Voyager I passed the orbital plane of Neptune and left our solar system. Within that time, there were no further messages sent. The crafts were still out in deep space, but NASA felt there would be no further messages sent, and they would not give an explanation that made sense.

Col. Bradfield, better known as Marsh, said that people around the world were now eager to listen for any signs of life or for signs that the Voyager mission crafts were intercepted. On October 12, 1992, Marsh said that NASA initiated the High Resolution Microwave Survey, which was a decade-long search by radio telescope scanning 10 million frequencies for any transmission by extraterrestrial intelligent life. The largest radio telescope was located in Aracebo, Puerto Rico. Less than one year later, Marsh was told that first-term Nevada Senator Richard Bryan successfully championed an amendment that terminated the project. I asked Marsh why this monumental research project that was approved overwhelmingly by several senators, congressman, and respected astronauts was terminated by the senator of a state that houses the most secret Air Force base in the world:

Area 51. According to Colonel Bradfield, the reason was we had made contact.

Marshall Bradfield was a 92-year-old man who, because of his rare form of cancer, chose to be transferred from a well-known military hospital in the east to MD Anderson Cancer Institute in Houston, Texas. It was at MD Anderson that he was accepted into a 12-week investigational protocol that was to attempt, as Col. Marsh put it, "to win by losing."

I met Marsh and his wife, Betty, as the ambulance pulled into our facility in Houston, Texas. They were a lovely couple, holding hands and with tears in their eyes. As they peered out the rear window of the ambulance, our eyes met and we accepted our paths in this combined journey. As the door of the ambulance opened, Marsh immediately asked, "Are you the doctor I was told was going to help me come to closure on several issues in my life—you know, forgiveness and self-love, essentially reviewing my life?"

"Well, I am Dr. Lerma and am honored to be caring for you, yet my concern is that I may not be able to help you bring closure to your issues before you pass."

"Then who?" Marsh asked incredulously.

"Do you really want to know?" I asked.

"Yes," Marsh replied.

"Well many of my patients tell me that God and his angels do the best job."

Marsh looked sharply at me, raised an eyebrow, and asked, "Do you believe that hogwash?"

"Yes, I do, sir."

I replied by lifting an eyebrow in return. After gazing off into the distance for several moments, he replied, "I don't know why I said that…but then maybe I do. That's a really long story that my wife and I could tell you if you are interested."

My curiosity peaked, and I immediately asked, *"Absolutely. When? Now?"*

Marsh looked at me as though he was sizing me up, hesitated a moment, and replied, "Well, I'm sure you have heard by now that I was in Roswell, New Mexico, when the reported flying saucer crashed on Mac Brazel's ranch." I recalled the rumors surrounding Marsh's arrival and replied, *"I did hear that you had worked in top-secret facilities but was unaware of your knowledge of the Roswell crash."*

I stepped back from the rear entrance of the ambulance to allow the attendants to assist Marsh and his wife out of the vehicle. Before being taken into the facility, Marsh smiled impishly, with what I would come to know as his signature expression—one cocked eyebrow—and said, "Well, why don't you come back later this evening after I have settled in and have eaten some tasty hospital food so I can give you the details? I promise you will not be disappointed. In fact, I think it would be prudent if you brought your pen and paper, or your laptop. I've already heard that you have written a book of your patients' lives and their death bed experiences, and I know my story will fit right in."

After finishing rounds and grabbing a quick dinner in the hospice dining room, I eagerly returned to his room that evening to find him relieved and thrilled that he finally was going to be able to tell his story. As I entered his room, he was lying in bed wearing a bomber jacket over his pajamas. He had laid out many of his medals and photos of his army buddies, his children, and his wife. He had already made a decision that this room would be his last stop, and he was trying to make it as homey and comfortable as possible. His wife was sitting in a chair at his side, a position that was both familiar and comforting for her, smiling with adoration. "Come on in, Doc. Sit down please. I think I am ready. I have reviewed the files in my mind. I have never written anything about that experience for fear of reprisal from the government." I sat down and opened my journal. As I flipped through the book looking for the first empty page, I paused momentarily on Matthew's and Katarina's stories, suddenly aware that Marsh was occupying the same room. With a tear beginning to role down my cheek, I looked up to meet Marsh's empathetic eyes. Was it possible that Marsh was already aware of Matthew's and Katarina's presence? Marsh took a deep breath, and thus began the most amazing story I have ever heard.

Marsh was born into a military family in Roswell, New Mexico, in 1923. As a teenager, he was already accustomed to military life, having traveled around the world with his parents.

Marsh had always desired the same type of life for himself, and joined the Army after December 7, 1941. Because Marsh had graduated at the top of his class, he was sent to West Point, where he graduated as a physicist six years later. Soon after his graduation he was sent to work with the Army Science and Technology division, where he worked on highly classified projects. I asked him if he had worked on propulsion systems, to which he replied dryly, "Like I said, I worked in the Science and Technology division of the Army."

In the summer of 1947, Marsh returned to Roswell to spend July 4th with his father and mother. Major thunderstorms rolled in that evening, squelching many festivities. Similar to many Roswellians, he went back home and spent the evening with his family. The following morning, the storms had dissipated, the sun was shining, and it appeared that it would be another hot day—that is, until Mac Brazel came knocking on the Bradfield door. Marsh recalled opening the door to let Mac in and immediately noted that he was quite flustered, yet with a sense of excitement and exuberance emanating from his being. Marsh replied, "Mac said he had heard that I was back in town for the holiday and wanted to visit. He did not seem to be aware that it was only 6:45 in the morning and that he had awakened us. This did not seem to deter him from urging me to come to his ranch immediately. Mac came to me because we had grown up together as boys in Roswell. He knew of my experience in the military and felt I would be excited as he was to see what was on his ranch."

Marsh dressed quickly, and he and Mac left in his pickup. As they drove to Mac's ranch, topping hill after hill, Mac began sharing what had occurred the night before and what he had found on his ranch. He thought he had heard a crash the night before, but had attributed it to the thunderstorm that had passed. It was not until the next morning, as he drove over his land, that he discovered hundreds of pieces of metal strewn over several hundred yards around the property. He described the metal pieces as being anywhere from a couple of inches to several feet in size, the largest of which sported an emblem that was very familiar to him. What was not familiar to him was the quality of the metal, which apparently had memory. In other words, he said that it was thin, like foil, and he could crunch it up only to see it expand back to its original shape in a few minutes. He told me he had seen geometrically shaped symbols on some of the metal fragments.

Marsh and Mac continued driving, swerving to avoid felled tree limbs and large mud puddles, arriving at an area that overlooked the field filled with the metallic debris. Marsh said that he jumped out of the truck immediately, and ran toward the field of debris, thinking that an airplane had crashed. He was looking for survivors, yet there was no evidence of fire or any odor of airplane fuel, which he was accustomed to smelling at an airplane crash around the airforce region. Around that time, several Army vehicles were seen traveling just northwest of the ranch. Marsh knew at that moment that something highly secure had crashed in this area and that the Army retrieval team had been called in. Marsh made note of several facts: the lack of airplane fuel on the property, the small size of the debris, the lack of engine parts, the lack of evidence of fire, and an incomplete emblem. With a cold chill running up his spine, he found the shape to be vague, but frighteningly familiar. As he pieced parts of the emblem together, it increasingly resembled the German Iron Cross, which Hitler used on his military vehicles and aircraft. Marsh felt twinges of fear deep in his gut, and knew that this incident had a much higher level of security than his clearance made him privy to, and as such he knew the consequences of being found in the area around the crash site.

Marsh asked Mac to take him home immediately, after which he called his commander at Wright-Patterson Air Force Base. Marsh was reluctant to make that name known to me because of the sensitivity of the situation, and its implications with regard to national security. Marsh commented that his commander was aware of the crash, and told him that the government had been planning a campaign of misinformation. After the war, the United States had recruited several German scientists to continue the research on which they had been working. One of those projects included the turbine engine as well as the use of electromagnetic energy for flight. Hitler's elite scientists had created the Haunebu 1 craft, which were saucer-like vehicles that reportedly employed this advanced technology toward the end of WWII.

One might remember these as the Foo Fighters, which pilots had observed flying next to them in battle during World War II. Marsh said he later learned that these craft were disassembled in Germany and reassembled at Wright-Patterson Air Force Base, from which many flights originated. In fact, months before the Roswell crash, there were already thousands of reports from civilians seeing saucer-shaped craft performing maneuvers yet unknown to our military. The news media was abuzz in the days and weeks following the crash. Seemingly overnight the Army had achieved its goal of convincing the public that this crash was a craft from another world. However, that was the farthest from the truth. The truth was that the United States had attained the technology through the German scientists' achievements. Marsh stated that it was imperative that our government maintain suppression of this technology from the public, so that our greatest enemy of that time, the Russians, could not obtain the technology and threaten our superiority as a world power.

By this time, Marsh was beginning to tire, and he asked if I would mind returning the following day. I said my good nights and promised that I would return bright and early. Upon reviewing his laboratory work the following morning, I realized that it revealed worsening anemia. Yet, as I walked in, I saw Marsh sitting on the side of his bed, looking just the opposite of what I had expected. He had a glow about him, a glorious smile on his face, and was appearing more alert than ever.

He immediately began to tell me that something incredible had happened the night after our discussion. He spoke of two bright entities in the shape of humans that stood at the doorway of his room. Although they did not speak, he did sense incredible love emanating from their being. It was this sense that opened his heart and allowed him to hear their voices, which told him they were there for his life review and guidance back to God. They told him that there was nothing to fear, and at that moment they allowed him to see his deceased parents and friends. Marsh explained that his parents seemed to have entered his room from a light projecting from the region of the spirits' chests. His parents seemed to walk out of the light and toward the right side of his bed, which faced the door. They appeared to be in the prime of their lives, smiling, and with looks of complete joy. They told him they loved him, had never left him, and that they had had similar experiences. Marsh asked me if this was purely delusional, and, if not, if it was commonly experienced by other patients. *"Absolutely!"* I replied. *"The vast majority of my patients have reported seeing angels or spiritual beings as you described, at the doorway around three to four weeks before their death. Moreover, those visions usually lasted anywhere from two to four seconds the first few weeks, increasing to hours in the last days of life."* This information reassured Marsh, as well as his wife, and allowed them both to breathe a deep sigh of relief that the end, indeed, would be comforting.

After six weeks of the intense treatment protocol, accompanied with a multitude of white cell and red cell progenitors, which were added to minimize the chemo-induced destruction of red and white cells, Marsh said, "If the cancer and the damn chemo doesn't kill me, then the 10-day-old burrito I ate last night will." I laughed with Marsh, as I knew laughter was the best medicine. Sadly, the fact was that there was no improvement after six weeks of harsh treatment.

"Thank God I was already bald, tall, and thin, and with white-blonde eyebrows and eyelashes. The chemo could not take much more. Most of my life, because of my body habitus and lack of hair, many people thought I was going through chemotherapy. In fact, the nurses who initially assessed me really thought I was just finishing up the protocol, and, when I told them I was just starting, well, their facial expressions were priceless. I was a tough old gizzard from the worst world war ever. Dr. Lerma, if I looked like this while fighting the Germans, well, I can only imagine what went through their minds as they saw a tall, thin, bald guy behind a 50-caliber gun. Dr. Lerma, I knew this poison was going to kill me and not cure me. This treatment is like the principles of war, often employing evil against evil, the consequences being tremendous loss of life on both sides, and the guilt and self-defeating convictions that follow.

"Other than the use of death and destruction to accomplish a goal, why not use something almost polar opposite, where life begets life? Is it possible that the human race has become satisfied and complacent with our ways to achieve peace and fight disease? Is it possible that 21st-century medicine, whose oath is to 'do no harm,' is resorting to fifth-century 'do harm tactics' to cure or fight diseases? I am sorry, but when a doctor says they will 'do no harm' to their patients, then injects a poison into their blood stream to kill or cripple the enemy, I believe they are hypocrites—total hypocrites. They should be ashamed of themselves for lying to their patients and especially for utilizing the barbaric and expensive treatments that only benefit the pockets of the drug companies.

"There needs to be a worldwide gathering of the most brilliant minds in medicine, mathematics, and physics to set a time period with which to find the cures to the most lethal diseases that plague the human race. While they are at it, they might as well eradicate hunger. Throughout the last 50 to 100 years, the United States has been able to achieve the seemingly impossible, when people come together for the same cause. One major example was when President Kennedy mandated that the United States land a man on the moon within 10 years. No one would have ever believed the human race could have accomplished this inconceivable endeavor.

"This 'do harm' mentality works well for the military, but not our medical profession. From the moment you shake hands with the doctor and his staff, they commence the 'do harm.' They first start by damaging your emotional and interpersonal self by not telling you what the numbers and percentages don't tell you. Their perceptions of those numbers are always skewed toward treatment, even when they are clearly futile. In addition, the drugs used do not specifically kill the cancer cells. In fact, they exterminate all good cells surrounding the malignancy. In the military we call that collateral damage and that's considered acceptable. I would never believe that this would be justifiable in medicine, where the mantra of 'do no harm' is to be held in their hearts and souls.

"Their meaning of quality of life is so far from 'city and country folks' perception. For the doctors, a satisfactory result of treatment is being alive. Just alive. Even if one is on a respirator, artificial feeding, poorly responsive, or confined to a bed or wheelchair, most physicians consider this result to be sufficient. To be kept alive to experience life in a comatose state or from a bed or wheelchair is not acceptable. Doctors should demand better treatment options or accept comfort medicine as a treatment option. Dr. Lerma, thank God that the American Board of Medical Specialties finally agreed that palliative medicine, or comfort medicine, was to be the latest sub-specialty."

Marsh believed that with the choice of treatments, aggressive or palliative, given to human beings, quality of life should be standard before one dies. He hoped that the medical industry (physicians and pharmaceuticals) would use their money to passionately search the cure for diseases that affect both large numbers and small groups of people. "If there is a God, I am sure he would want our scientists to be using their brains and hearts to develop treatments that would cure diseases and relieve suffering and pain."

I was taken aback by his comments regarding contemporary medicine and the lack of the "do no harm" mentality. This certainly allowed me to reevaluate the oath I took to help relieve suffering.

"Dr. Lerma, during my tenure as a physicist with the Army, I had access to very sensitive information, and some side-chatting, of course. In the early 1970s, I got wind that there existed a protocol written by the powers that be in the United States that dealt with securing the cure within the Research and Development Division of the Army, and then determining the immediate and long-lasting effects of the drug on the economy, religions, and political governments of the world. If the results showed that there would be a negative impact on our economy and jobs at home, then the cure would be concealed. If this is true, this is beyond criminal.

"One more thing: Isn't it funny how most of those high powered doctors never seem to mention the 'C' word as they are explaining the treatment for your cancer. No, I don't mean cancer— I mean cure. That is because when it comes down to using investigational drugs, one's chances for a cure are worse than winning the lottery twice in a row, on Christmas Day on a leap year. Why do we even do it, Dr. Lerma? I believe that, in the backs of our minds, what we believe heaven and God to be is far from what we were taught. I believe most decisions are left up to us. There is no God sitting on a throne, watching, waiting, and dictating. I think God is inside us all, and, for this reason, it is up to all of us to make the changes for the better, always remembering that for every choice there are consequences, some good and some bad.

The constant of both effects being knowledge. The goal, I believe, is to learn from our choices and ultimately teach the lessons learned to our children, in the hopes of making their lives and the lives of others more fruitful and peaceful. Feeling entitled or waiting for someone to do it for you will only upset you and make you anxious; everyone who is mentally and physically healthy just needs to stop complaining and being complacent, and just do what their hearts and soul's desire; those who cannot need help. Dr. Lerma, in a dream I had last night, I saw my souls desires, which were God's as well, and when I chose to pursue them, I saw God smile and reach out to give me the keys to the doors that led to the treasures he placed in my heart. I strongly believe that, to achieve enduring peace and love, all one has to do is take the first step forward toward one's divine-driven dreams."

Marsh was definitely angry at his suffering and the suffering in the world. This was understandable. Yet, what Marsh was saying was completely from his heart and true. To many he was tough as nails, but all I saw and heard was a man who was full of love for God and humanity.

The cancer was now spreading rapidly and with intense aggression. Colonel Bradfield had decided to surrender to the enemy. He believed God was calling him back home, and the cancer was dictating his timed departure. Similar to most lifers in the military, he remained stoic, strong, and ready for his next journey—one he hoped would no longer involve wars, hatred, destruction, and devastation. He was truly remorseful for his past, and felt he needed to reconcile much about what he felt were sins against the entire world. To try to achieve peace, and love within himself, he needed to do something that meant fostering hope, peace, and love in the world, even if it meant breaking his oath.

Colonel Marsh worked as a particle physicist. He had worked at such facilities as Los Alamos and Wright-Patterson Air Force Base, which were known to be among the most highly secured research facilities in the United States. Because Los Alamos was involved in the original atomic bomb experiments was it possible that Marsh had been exposed to radiation during those times and was now living with the consequences of that exposure? Having worked at Brooke Army Medical Center in San Antonio and Audie Murphy Veterans Hospital during my residency, I saw and spoke with many soldiers who had been part of the nuclear experiments in Los Alamos and were now dying from rare forms of cancer. How many people died as a result of those experiments? Was it worth the cost? One soldier queried, "How much evil must one do to accomplish good?"

After several days of intimate discussion regarding the government's conspiratorial campaign of disinformation, along with his life experience with cancer and its treatment, his disease process finally steered him into a semi-comatose state. He had continued seeing his parents and friends nightly since that first day that they had appeared. They aided in his life review, which included some of his more questionable actions during his military career. As far as being a husband and father, he was always loving and true to his wife and children. Because of his under-standing and wisdom, which came from a place of love and for-giveness, his life review would not be as intense. The day of his death, Marsh, who had been in a coma for five days, opened his eyes and asked to speak with his wife and me. With an incredible smile upon his face, and his eyes now as blue as the Aegean Sea, he told us both, with a raised eyebrow, that a young boy on a dolphin, who previously died in this room, had shown him our lives, past, present, and future, and that it was the most beautiful sight he had ever seen. It was exactly as he remembered the angels telling him.

As his breathing tired, so did his ability to speak. At that point, his wife and I took his hands and recited an Our Father and a Hail Mary. Marsh's cocked eyebrow slowly relaxed as did all but one of his facial muscles. As we finished the Hail Mary, Marsh's breathing slowed, and he peacefully faded away. All that was left was a beautiful smile I was all too familiar with. Similar to many of my patients who breathed their last breath with a smile, I knew Marsh was reacting to the sight of our Creator and all of his feathered angels. Marsh's smile was clearly conveying jubilation, exultation, and sheer ecstasy at the glorious sight of victory.

Doctor's Notes

Neil Armstrong, Gordon Cooper, Edgar Mitchell, President Ronald Reagan, President Bill Clinton, and President Jimmy

Carter, as well as millions of Americans, wanted to believe. My newest patient, by the name of Colonel Marshal Bradfield, *did* believe, and, before he died from a rare form of radiation-induced cancer, he decided to disclose something of enormous importance to the world. I will never forget his most fascinating confession.I was taken back by the last few words Marsh left me with. Was it possible that the boy on the dolphin was Matthew? Did this 9-year-old sage, who transitioned in this same room almost one year to the date, help Marsh transition to the next realm? If so, had he helped all other patients in this same room? Whatever the answer, I knew that Matthew was doing exactly what he did while on this planet: helping others find God. This was simply incredible.

Several days before his departure from this world, Marsh began to discuss how the angels were guiding him toward closure. Marsh explained that his compulsive personality made it difficult to accept his disease process. He wanted to know how it happened, why it happened, and what he needed to do to claim victory. As a soldier, Marsh viewed every obstacle in life as a battle. He had it in his mind to be victorious once more. He told me the following day that he had learned his victory was beyond this world and, had he known what was shown to him by the angels, he would have lived his life less compulsive and anxious.

"Will you tell me more about your life review?"

"Dr. Lerma, had I truly believed where I was going after this world, I would have lived a life less compulsive and anxious. I would have lived it more fully and with much less worry."

"Why would you worry less?"

"Because God and his angels are continuously, and I mean continuously, watching out for us. I never knew how intricately balanced and cared for our lives are. When I was shown the multiple times God saved me from sure death throughout my life, I knew my cancer was his way of bringing me back home. I had finally understood that we were just passing through this world and on our way toward a place that dreams are made off. The angels told me that the free, secure, and ecstatic feelings our flying dreams leave us with are very similar to what it feels like in heaven."

"Do you sense heaven with the five senses we are given on Earth?"

"You are given more than five senses to experience heaven. I believe it's on the order of infinity. In other words, the more you understand about God and his plan, the more intense the experience. The thing about God's plan is its eternal in nature. That means you will spend eternity experiencing multiple levels of love, joy, compassion, forgiveness, and even laughter. So, the feelings are constantly changing. Nothing in heaven stays the same."

"What do you mean 'nothing in heaven stays the same'?"

"Its nothing horrible, Dr. Lerma. All I mean is that love continuously grows. As long as you continually seek to know with love, the experiential feeling will eternally expand. It is simply magnificent."

"What if you choose to stay away from God?"

"Fortunately, God has a plan for even those lost souls. He will never forget anyone. There is something sad about this choice though. While one is lost in their created hell, the same rules apply. In other words, if these people choose to experience anger, hatred, or sadness, they will fall deeper and deeper into their own snare. The only way out is to feel some bit of compassion or love for someone else. Since nothing stays the same, one will continuously be maturing in whatever emotion they opt for."

"So, God is always helping us?"

"Sure. Even in the hell we conjure for ourselves. That's what he does. He will not stop until his plan is fulfilled. One of the sad things about God's way is that he has to enter the hell we created to save us. That's how much he loves us."

As I thought about what Marsh said, I felt an incredible sadness for God. I wanted so much to make things better. The reality was that I could not force people to change their dark and somber ways. Marsh said the only way to effectively change someone toward love and light was through prayer. Marsh said that God depended highly on our selfless petitions to help our fellow man and his lost souls. I would never view prayer the same.

Marsh commented that everyone on this planet is constantly being protected from destruction. This is done in order to provide the incalculable lessons human life has to offer. Marsh comments, "I'm asking for healing and I am being shown the 30 times God has already healed me. The time has come to accept the way I will die or move onward to the next realm. No one is meant to live forever on this planet, and now I see the fear that kept me in the familiar environment of earth and the heavenly realm that is our perfected home."

"How would you describe heaven?"

"Dr. Lerma, there are no pain, no diseases, and no depression on the other side. Tell everyone not to worry and to always desire to be with God, especially when he is calling us back home. Many people choose to battle the inevitable, and this only leads to unnecessary lessons. If people could simply open their hearts to the infinite possibilities God has given us, our lives and deaths would be much easier. Had I learned my lessons earlier, I could have passed away in my sleep. Still, the comfort I am feeling now is remarkable."

"What other advice do you have for the world?"

"We must strive to become transparent. We must open ourselves and love ourselves enough to become evident. We should not hold on to secrets, as they only serve our personal and selfish motives. Random acts of kindness and selfless prayers are the key. It is these two last acts that create miracles."

Dialogue About Life on Other Planets

I found it very interesting that Marsh had commented that NASA knew likely existed on other planets in our solar system and galaxy. In fact, many of NASA and JPL's space missions from the 1970s had proven this age-old question. For national security and financial reasons, they were kept from sharing this incredible finding with the world. Marsh went on to explain about the possibility of past life on Mars.

"When the Viking Explorer's first pictures of Mars returned the media carried one picture in particular: the face on Mars in the region known as Cydonia. Scientists were hoping that this was evidence of life on Mars. The face of Cydonia had eyes, a mouth, nose, and ears that were suggestive of a human-like face. Predictions, which included size, shape, and distance of eyebrows, lips, nostrils, iris, and ears were made by NASA scientists to eliminate bias. The key to proving these predictions was sending a second mission that would take highly defined digital images of Cydonia. Thus, the Spirit, or Unity, and Phoenix missions were launched, which returned images that proved the face on Mars to have been intelligently created."

Marsh stated that, although most people are not aware of this finding, it is not only true, but will be divulged in the near future. He went on to tell me that water was also discovered on Mars in the 1980s, yet the European Space Agency (ESA) and NASA finally agreed to release the information in 2008. What else did NASA and the ESA know about and not tell us? According to Marsh, the last missions to Mars proved, through the digital images, that foliage, and fossils exist on Mars today. In addition, on the unnatural mesa 1 kilometer next to Cydonia, images outlined on the surface around Cydonia resembling a child, an Egyptian goddess, marine animals, as well as glass tubes were found. The ESA reported that these glass tubes were found to connect several of the above-mentioned structures, which were reportedly interlaced metallic support beams.

I asked Marsh how something so monumental could be kept from the public. He said that it was not necessarily kept from the public, as it is located on many sites throughout the Internet. In other words, it is being buried until they are ready to reveal it to the public. He continued and stated that this revelation has many stages. He said the first stage will occur when the Vatican announces, "It is okay to believe in extra-terrestrial."

In the summer of 2008, the Vatican did announce that it was possible that extra-terrestrials likely existed on other planets, and that this was in keeping with the Bible. Interestingly, the same day the Vatican announced the acceptance of the possibility of extra-terrestrials, the British government also revealed many of their X-files having to do with advanced aerial technology, including anti-gravity systems and knowledge of extra-terrestrial biological entities (EBEs). Indeed, Colonel Marsh Bradfield was correct. Since this announcement by the Vatican and Britain, it is now known that the moon, Bellona, exploded 3.5 million years ago, which was about the same time that the first human was discovered by anthropologists. Was this a coincidence? Marsh said, "No." He continued to challenge my belief system by stating that humans lived on Bellona and were well aware of their planet's impending natural demise, thus forcing them to relocate to the next most habitable planet: Earth.

Prior to Hitler's reign, his top archeologists and anthropologists were sent on a very specific mission, which eventually led to the most remarkable discovery in man's history: evidence of an ancient civilization that included human remains, and tablets that held information of their advanced technical knowledge and existence, including objects and materials that appeared to belong to some sort of advanced aerial craft. This information that Marsh was easily recounting was difficult for me to reconcile with my scientific and spiritual background, yet there was something in his voice and demeanor that told me there was truth in his comments. The research I had undertaken to prove or disprove in the least kept me interested.

It is interesting that Hitler's rapid advancement in the fields of aeronautics and physics seemed to coincide with their reported archaeological findings. Even more interesting was the fact that within one to two years after WWII, the U.S. exponential advancement in the fields of aeronautics and physics was more than coincidental. It was under Project Paperclip that the U.S. military brought in most of Hitler's top scientists into Wright-Patterson Air Force Base in Toledo, Ohio. It was nearly 18 months after WWII when thousands of U.S. citizens began to observe saucer-shaped craft around Toledo, Ohio, and as far as Roswell, New Mexico. The question I was left with related to how many of these aerial craft were terrestrial versus extraterrestrial. One thing was clear to me: the United States does have and operate aerial craft that exceeds speeds of 40,000 miles an hour and performs maneuvers beyond our current understanding.

I have to say that everything that I have heard with regard to extra-terrestrial conspiracies involving Germany, the Vatican, and the U.S. government is mind-boggling, to say the least. However, when I think about how Marsh spoke of the countless loving spiritual entities, including souls he said that once lived on other planets in our Universe, which were present around his bed, I am finally left with the reconciliation of the one common factor during one's transition: No matter what, we are all ultimately unified by the one source—God.

7

Mary Magdalene

Mary Magdalene came and told the disciples that she had seen the Lord. And He had spoken these things to her.

—John 20:18

Grace Livingston was a 102-year-old woman who entered my life almost five years ago. Grace was a refined woman from the South; her family was very well known in the political world, as well as during the Civil War. You see, her distant relatives were Confederate officers, and their love for the South continued through the subsequent generations and now flowed through Grace's blood. She experienced the best and the worst of America, and had outlived most of her children and all of her siblings. Grace was diagnosed with stage four pancreatic cancer, and she was given less than six weeks to live; according to Grace, this was the best news she had heard in more than 40 years. She looked deep into my eyes and told me that the worst part of her life was outliving her children and wondering whether God would ever take her back home.

Many of my previous patients who had lived to be more than 100 years old have made similar comments and felt that they had committed some horrible sins that God would not forgive. Their punishment was living on this planet well beyond the average age and beyond all of their friends and family. She was transferred to the hospice for end-of-life care and pain management. When we first met, her pain was written all over her face, but her stoic nature kept her from admitting her discomfort. It was obvious with a pulse of 110 and notable grimacing, as well as a protruding tumor from her abdomen that her pain was among the worst I had seen. I immediately had the nurse administer intravenous morphine as well as an anti-anxiety agent.

However, just as the nurse was about the administer the medication, Grace refused. She wanted to be as alert as possible throughout the remainder of her life so that she could converse with the few family members she had still living, as well as God and his angels. This was quite difficult for me to watch, but, because she was of sound mind and body, I had to respect her wishes. She was very grateful that we respected her wishes, and, after she settled in, she asked for her afternoon cup of Earl Gray tea, which she had grown accustomed to.

When her tea arrived, she politely asked me to sit down and join her for a cup. I obliged, as I wanted to get to know Grace better. By now I knew that most of my patients who came to terms with their disease process and knew that they were in their last weeks of life were open to discussing not only their life review, but also their very personal experiences. You see, most people wanted confirmation from a nonjudgmental source that their life was not lived in vain. For Grace, I became that source. Grace explained that she was a very strong-willed woman and all of her life she had fought for women's rights, including the right to vote. She became very close friends with Rosa Parks, who is known for defying the discriminatory practices of her time. When Grace heard of Rosa Parks's determined nature, she immediately set out to help her achieve her goals to abolish segregation. This eventually came to pass, and Rosa Parks became an icon, not only for the black population, but for all women.

Rosa's and Grace's desire to help women was the bond that cemented their friendship. Years later, Rosa Parks died and Grace explained that she was told Rosa began to see her parents and other deceased loved ones around her bed, comforting her with knowledge and visions of heaven and God's plan. Weeks earlier, Grace had a vision of Rosa, who told her that her life, much like hers, would work out in perfection. Rosa went on to explain to Grace that she was born to give birth to the advent of desegregation and union of people of different colors. Her last words to Grace were, "Do not stop believing in God, and understand that his plan may appear quite difficult at times, but I can see the perfection in it now that I am about to go home."

"I will be there by your side, Grace, when your time comes."

Grace's condition continued to progress, but somehow her pain decreased dramatically throughout the ensuing days. I was not quite sure, as a physician, how this could be, as her tumor was now much larger and compressing nerves, and she was only on Tylenol. Grace replied with an exhilarating smile, "Dr. Lerma, the angels have taken my pain away."

"How is that so, Grace?"

"Difficult to say, but somehow they get in my mind and make me forget through the beautiful images they are revealing to me."

"What kind of images are you seeing, Grace?"

She went on to tell me that they would take her spirit from her body in the evenings and travel around the Earth looking at the most beautiful creations on this planet. She described visiting the pyramids of Giza, Machu Picchu in Peru, and Antarctica, as well as many schools and homes where people of different races and colors were all playing and living together. She said that this was probably the most incredible sight she had seen, as it showed her that what she had fought for all of her life was now occurring. I asked her if the angels had shown her heaven or hell, to which she stated that there was no hell like what we were taught to believe.

She explained what thousands of my patients had told me, and that was that hell was merely a self-separation from God. This self-separation, she stated, was due to people's inability to love and forgive themselves. This lack of self-love and self-forgiveness, again, was mentioned by many of my patients, and always reverted back to the fact that people in our society and churches were giving power to guilt and furthering the purpoted false existence of hell. Grace said that the angels told her that not much had changed in several thousand years with regard to man's self-hatred and self-condemnation.

Grace was told that this would change one day as wiser souls were being reborn into our world to lead us into our next evolution of sorts: Humans would be transparent with extrasensory abilities as well as clairvoyance, all of which would aid toward this new, loving movement. Interestingly, of all the visions and angelic messages she was given, what impressed me the most were her vision and collaboration with Mary Magdalene. Similar to thousands of patients before her, she saw the spirits of deceased loved ones; however, her review differed, in that it was a detailed account of the role of women leaders of the family, church, and world. She began with her story of attempting to stop the segregation of the disenfranchised, as well as opposing war and hatred. When Mary Magdalene finally appeared to Grace she appeared as a beautiful woman with long, flowing dark hair and what appeared to be a dark blue robe. She appeared one night next to Grace's bed and explained who she was and that her life review would consist of understanding the plight of women from the time of Jesus, as this subject matter was vital to her peaceful transition. Because Grace was Jewish, she was not quite aware of Mary's life, but during the following days, she ended up knowing more about her life than what was mentioned in the Bible.

Mary stated that there were four gospels in the Bible, yet her gospel, which was written by her closest friends, was purposefully omitted by the Council of Nicea around AD 320. It was obvious that men, even around the time of Jesus, did not view women as their equal, and thus they could not have a gospel placed in the Bible that would not only show that women were equal to men, but more importantly, would show that Mary was Jesus's confidante. In fact, Jesus appeared to Mary first, and not the other disciples. Grace told me that this is where the story of Mary ends in the Bible and where it continues in her gospel. When Jesus appeared to Mary, this was the defining moment for Mary, but also the defining moment for all women, past, present, and future. It was during that profound encounter that Jesus explained to Mary that he wanted his church to move toward self-enlightenment through self-love and self-forgiveness.

Of interest, the rest of the disciples were known to have been hiding in one of their homes. They were upset and frightened after Jesus died, because of what might happen to him. Mary and Serome felt secure that Jesus would protect them, so they went out, as it states in the Bible, to the tomb where Jesus lay. After Jesus appeared to Mary, she proceeded to the hiding place of the disciples and told them that Jesus had appeared to her and told her about enlightenment. According to the gospel, Mary answered and said, "What is hidden from you, I will proclaim to you." Mary reportedly made this statement after Peter asked her what Jesus had told her. Peter went on to ask her why she was so calm, especially with the Roman soldiers threatening to kill anyone who knew Jesus. He went on to ask her if she knew something they didn't. Grace explained that Mary told her what she had told the disciples. She said that Jesus spoke of a different way of understanding his death and resurrection. She said that Jesus' death symbolized the death of the world and the resurrection symbolized our new body. For one's salvation it was not so much about the dying process, sickness, and eventual understanding that we live forever without pain; it was about enlightenment. What is important was that Jesus was a teacher, and, although his death was very sad from a human perspective, he wanted us to know the real joy. This joy came from truly understanding his teaching from within and not as much from the outside.

Mary went on to say that he wanted us to be leery of men who teach their own interpretation of Jesus's death. Many could be right, but it would be easier to trust the truth within ourselves. You see, the kingdom of God is within all of us and, because of this, Jesus lives within us, and is constantly guiding us and speaking to us. Many of us choose not to listen to this gut feeling, but many others do. Either way, God experiences the choices we make. Mary told Grace that the gut feeling she had with regard to helping stop prejudice despite the opposition she came across was God talking to her and leading her. If more of us would just take a chance and listen to this gut instinct, our lives could rapidly change toward a joyous existence. If we were to hit critical mass with regard to this understanding, then the whole world would change.

Even though this might appear to most humans as an impossible feat, God has promised that it will manifest itself within the next hundred years. Grace explained to me that the "gut feeling" Mary speaks about would tell you when something is right, it is right, and when something is wrong, it is wrong. In order to learn this, each individual must take time to learn who he or she is most often by living alone or being independent in order to become whole. It is at this time that one gets to understand our sinful self, which is the ego, and our higher self, which is connected to God. One could say one is negative and the other is positive; however, together they make us whole. I guess this is what God might have meant when he said, "When two or more are gathered, there am I in their midst."

Grace said that we have to love ourselves no matter how hateful we are, because the knowledge of this love is what brings about enlightenment. It was this inner understanding that Jesus spoke to Mary about. In old Buddhist texts there is mention of a highly spiritual individual by the name of Enoch who was a man from Galilee. This man was apparently Jewish and in his late teens, desired to learn what Buddha was told by God. It was during this period of time that Enoch, who Mary says was Jesus, spread the news of enlightenment, something that Buddha had learned almost 600 years before. Interestingly, there is no mention of the years of Jesus' life after his birth and up until around his death. Mary told Grace that there are many texts around the world in existence today with knowledge of his experiences during those years.

When Mary went back to see the apostles, she eventually told them about the principle that Jesus had told her about. Peter and the other apostles had difficulty understanding this principle as it appeared, at face value, self-centered and inconsiderate of others. Thus, when the Romans asked who the leaders of this new Christian movement were, Mary, along with Serame and other women, who were devoutly involved in spreading Jesus' word were intentionally removed from the list. It was then that the so-called conspiracy against women began. So Mary wanted to thank Grace for helping elevate women back to a level where they were now respected by society. In fact, it took just more than 2,000 years to allow women to be back in the political arena, as well as in the hierarchy of the church. In fact, we had the first woman run for president and a black man, who has been elected president of the United States. Grace said that Jesus appeared at the foot of her bed, knelt in humility, and washed her feet. With tears in her eyes from total joy and love, she knew now what she wished everyone knew: that our loving Creator has given us the amazing gift of free will. With one last tear rolling down her right cheek, she reached out toward the foot of her bed, leaned forward, smiled, and said, "I'm ready to go home, Jesus."

Minutes later she fell asleep and slowly faded away into the light.

Upon hearing Grace's words, it brought back memories of all the patients who had told me that self-love and self-gratitude were the key to a peaceful transition, but, more importantly, the key to accepting Jesus as our savior. Grace told me that Mary would appear nightly, for what she felt was days and even weeks, yet in reality it was only about two to four hours. Here was that time difference again, much like the Bible, where 1,000 years is equal to one day.

Doctor's Notes and More Dialogue With Grace

Grace Livingston was such an impressive, enthusiastic, and strongly admired woman. I will never forget the work she so passionately pursued when fighting for woman's civil liberties and equality, as well as being resolute in desegregating schools, churches, and transportation in the south. It was obvious that God had chosen her to rekindle the desire within all souls that which God desired himself: unconditional love for everyone.

I researched the life of Mary Magdalene, and in the process I interviewed several theologians and archaeologists that were familiar with Mary's life and the gospel of Mary. I wanted to compare what Grace recanted about Mary with what was written in historic texts. I not only discovered that what Grace was telling me about Mary was fairly accurate, but that secular Christian religions were debunking the archaeologists findings as fast as new information and relics were being discovered. A dying Catholic priest once told me that one must question the person who claims to know the whole truth, whereas the person who only claims to be searching for the truth within is to be trusted. Sound advice.

The following are more messages that Grace was given by the angels and Mary about enlightenment. With regard to Jesus' Second Coming, the angels commented that this was meant to be taken literally and metaphorically. His Second Coming was not to be viewed as an apocalyptic event, but a personal revelation. He was to be sought within our souls and not in the clouds. There is no doubt that he will return as promised in the Bible; however, he reportedly told Mary that, to understand this promise, each individual would have to attain enlightenment where desire and suffering are transcended. Upon this achievement, the spirit of Jesus manifests itself within our very essence. Because Mary understood that she needed to exist above and apart from the material world, and with this understanding, Jesus appeared to her first and not the other disciples. Most disciples knew that Mary had a very special relationship with Jesus and respected her immensely. These disciples yearned to hear what Jesus had told Mary, so she explained his new teaching, and they quickly learned this principle and experienced the second apparition of Jesus Christ. It was a century or so after the death of Jesus that man's primordial desire for the warrior mentality initiated the eradication of any mention of female leaders in the church and teachers of Christ's enlightenment philosophy. Most were eventually imprisoned or even put to death.

Grace emphasized that her understanding from Mary was that Jesus' teachings were not solely about eternal life, but more centered on wisdom and living a life in accordance with enlightenment, where less is more. This is why Catholic priests take the vow of poverty. This allows them to concentrate not on things of this world, but on things important to the next world.

According to Mary, the apostles Peter and Andrew were outraged that Jesus appeared to her first and did not believe he would confide in a woman without the rest of the apostles being present. One of the theologians I spoke to read a passage from the gospel of Mary that reportedly quotes Peter. "Did he speak with a woman in private with our knowing it? Did he choose her over us?" Another disciple quickly calmed the uproar and addressed Peter. "We should not fight with each other and instead do what the Savior told us, and that is to preach his teachings."

Engrossed in every word and syllable that came from Grace's mouth, I continued to write down what she was being told and shown by God's angels along with Mary. Grace said that Peter was the founding father of the Catholic Church, and it was well known that he felt that he was playing second fiddle to Mary. After all, she was the one who understood enlightenment, and as such knew what Jesus was about. Peter represented the necessary counterpart, which was motivated by pride, guilt, and fear. After all, Peter denied Jesus three times, thus representing most humans as well as the Catholic Church.

Because the kingdom of God was within, this represented the true church where God was the preacher. People would begin to understand his teachings despite being persecuted, and not by evil outside the church, but by evil inside the church. I continued to be in awe of the revelations Grace and her angels were providing.

She went on to say that this was the actual message from Fatima that was given in the 1990s, but not in its totality. I asked her why the Vatican did not reveal the entire message. Her response: because of fear. Essentially the same reason the rabbis did not tell their flock that Jesus appeared to them after he died and revealed his true essence.

Grace said that one of the larger angels, around 10 feet and golden to maroon in color, said that, even back in the times of Jesus, man was controlled by fear, guilt, and power, but our Creator's plan would play out in loving perfection for reconciliation. Several theologians remarked that the Gospel of Mary revealed a stunning reversal of roles in the early Christian church, where Mary, a woman, was the Church leader and Peter was second in command. In these old texts, it is obvious that there was an ancient power struggle, or a desire to become whole, between man and woman. It is much like the struggle we constantly experience between our self-defeating and unintelligent ego and our highly intelligent, loving, and self-sacrificing spiritual self. This battle has endured for centuries and is expressed in 1 Timothy 2:12: "I permit no woman to teach or to have authority over a man. She is to keep silent."

The theologians I spoke to commented on Pope Gregory, who reportedly wiped out any record of woman church leaders and diminished their roles dramatically. They went on to describe that in AD 180, the Bishop of Leon, Araneus, permanently removed the Gnostic Gospels of Thomas and Philip, both of whom spoke of individual enlightenment. Bishop Araneus did this, because he wanted to streamline the Bible by calling for a single Bible where he suggested that a list of certain books not be considered for admission. Historians and theologians felt that many Gnostic books were omitted because their teachings gave the individual too much power. In the fourth or fifth century, Christianity became more about control of the masses rather than enlightening them.

Mary to the Christian Church was proof that Jesus would forgive a prostitute and outcasts. Christian leaders used the fact that Jesus saved a "woman" who ultimately defeated the Gnostics and female church leaders. They essentially turned Mary into a prostitute and were able to condemn her Gospel or teachings as heretical. Overall, the angels told Grace that Jesus entrusted Mary with the most sacred message—a message about finding the one God within.

I know that many of my patients who are able to speak at the end of their lives described heaven as being within. For Grace, she spoke of the light not coming from the corner of the room, but from within her soul. "To find salvation, our Creator is to be sought within."

8 The Return of Misty

It was a sell-out crowd at the Frank Erwin Center in Austin, Texas, where the Eagles and Cougars were fighting it out to determine who would play Dallas for the state title in women's high school basketball. The score was 88 to 86, Cougars on top. The Eagles had the ball, in the fourth quarter with five seconds remaining, and the crowd was going crazy. "Misty, Misty, Misty," the crowd cheered, hoping that the Eagles' star player would get a chance to sink a three pointer for the win. The end of the game would be history in the making, as neither team had ever made it to regionals, let alone to the state championship. Misty and her teammates ran out onto the floor. Misty said the rest was happened like it was in slow motion.

"The ball was thrown to me in the two-point range, and I caught it. Not hearing the crowd now, I stepped backward, crossed the three-point line, and shot the ball. The crowd quieted for what appeared to be an eternity,

I closed my eyes, and then I heard a roar coming from the Eagles' sideline. The noise grew louder and louder as I began to open my eyes. The entire court was now filled with students, media, my teammates, and my mom. 'Mom, I did it. It was like the angels took the ball from my hands and guided it into the net to win the came. Mom, I can hardly stand it.' I was then lifted by my teammates and carried around the floor. The arena was filled with utter joy. When they presented me with the game-winning ball, I looked at my mom and said, 'This is for you! This ball belongs to you! For never giving up on life, or us, even after we lost Dad, Grandma, and Grandpa in a car accident three years ago. You are the best, Mom, hands down."

Misty told me this surreal experience was like something out of a movie and the script couldn't have been written any better. "This had to have been God-driven," Misty emphasized.

While sitting at the foot of the bed listening to Misty, I purposely glanced to the wall behind her, which was full of pictures and memorabilia; I was drawn immediately to her senior picture. The young woman I saw in the picture was like a model: tall, beautiful, blue-eyed with long, dark hair. What was in front of me was a mere resemblance of the woman in the picture. Misty was now reduced to weighing less than 90 pounds, her skin drawn and pale, her long hair now sparse. I saw Misty's eyes tearing as she looked down, reminded by my facial expression of how she once looked. She was now dying of terminal bone cancer. The chemotherapy and radiation were no longer effective, and thus she was placed in my care.

I met her mother, Mary, and younger sister, Tabetha, who were as beautiful and loving as Misty. Having read her chart hours before I took over her case, I knew that the cancer was one more horrific thing to add to the list of losses. About three years before, her father and maternal grandparents were instantly killed in a head-on collision as they were being taken home after Thanksgiving dinner. Because it was cold that night, their father insisted that they stay home with Mom while he took Mommo and Popo home. This amount of loss and pain was unfathomable, and it showed for the first few months after the accident, because they could not adjust to this heart-wrenching tragedy.

After Misty, Tabetha, and Mary all had visitations from their father and grandparents on the same night while getting ready for bed, the message given to each of them was amazingly similar. The children both ran out of their rooms heading to see their mother. As they entered her bedroom, they saw their mommy kneeling next to her bed crying and holding her hands up in the air in thanksgiving and praise to God. When the children's tearful eyes met with their mother's, they all knew instantly that all of them had the same vision at the same time.

After Mary walked into the room, I told her we were reminiscing about Misty's basketball days, as well as that fateful day. Interested in our topic, Mary joined in and explained that the visions they all had were eerily similar. They all described Dad, Popo, and Mommo as being surrounded by a translucent, white light that emanated peace as well as their individual messages.

The messages spoke of reassurance that they were in a beautiful place and would always be around to help and eventually come to bring them back home.

The message had an ominous tone toward the end, as it spoke of never losing hope, no matter how tough things got. They were told to remember that they were specifically chosen to help many lost souls as God graced them with undying love and faith. This is what it is ultimately all about, and, before we are born, some souls are so dedicated to the cause that the life-altering lessons are beyond human understanding. They were reminded that, at the end of the day, the purpose was to achieve an awakening to the God within us in order to find true peace and love first, followed by helping our fellow man achieve this same state of being, where power is unlimited and miracles occur. Misty also understood that, to obtain this power, one has to be brutally honest with oneself. One starts by making clear to oneself who we were and why we do what we do, be it hatred or love, fear or strength, chaos or peace, and making the appropriate changes in our total life. This could be daunting, and many give up. However, sooner or later, one sets out to accomplish it, often with the help of higher-level souls in the human form, or angelic spirits or deceased family members. Human souls that have recently become enlightened move to assist others in attaining this gift from God.

Misty told me that her dad spoke of different ways to help these lost souls realize enlightenment. Some of the ways may involve becoming a martyr. Others are even more costly. It is an extremely complicated process that demands the guidance of God. He made this stipulation to assure that we would not choose a way beyond one's mental and spiritual capability. If this occurred, it could be disastrous for both souls. This is why God has the last say in what the soul chooses. His love for us ensures will never be given more than what we can handle, and thus protect us from self-annihilation.

Misty's father told her that his family's choice to save other souls from destruction involved such deep emotional pain and suffering. To try to balance this pain, God gave the power to appear to the survivors of great loss. This brought much-needed comfort and solace, as well as sanity to be able to continue the plan of salvation of all lost souls. She remembers her dad saying, "Honey, we were chosen out of our free will long ago to help raise the level of humanity for eternity. Mary and the children told me that, from that day forward, they understood their calling and were honored."

This was so profound and beyond what I could understand.

Were they just rationalizing as a mental defense mechanism to cope with the trauma? Were they having a collective hallucination initiated by the mother? All I know is that my heart was tearing in two for Misty, Mary, and Tabetha. I wish I had the power they spoke of to go back to that fateful night and affect the outcome by manipulating a one-time event to alter the rest. God is right: This was too complex to make all possibilities fall into a peaceful and loving place. Only God could and would want to carry out this feat.

Misty's disease progressed quite rapidly throughout that week, and she was in severe bone pain from the cancer, but remained at peace. She was now seeing her father, grandparents, and loving spirits and guides. She would converse with me about her visions, but those conversations were quite limited, because she was sleeping 20 hours a day. On the sixth day, I entered the room and found Mary crying and pleading with God not to take her. "Please God, not yet. Pleeease!" Mary exclaimed. When I heard the crying, it was unmistakable. I had heard it before and knew it was coming from the depths of her soul. I had flashbacks of all the moms of deceased children who cried with such fervor. The tone was so powerful that it could have penetrated concrete and metal walls.

I gently placed my stethoscope over her chest and listened for a heartbeat for several minutes. I pronounced her dead at 12:50 p.m. I held Mary tight as she cried inconsolably. People from other rooms felt her pain and were all crying. I left Mary alone with Misty, and after 15 minutes I went back in with the nurse to check on her and found Mary on top of Misty shaking her to come back. Misty's cold, lifeless body moved like a rag doll. Incredibly, Mary said she was breathing again and she could hear her moan. Sure enough, Misty was breathing again and had a faint pulse. She had color in her face from the blood flow, but not much. She finally opened her eyes and slowly sounded some words. It sounded like she was saying, "Let me go. Let me go, Mom."

Mary replied, "Honey don't go. Please don't leave me. Tell God to let you stay. Oh, honey, please."

I pulled Mary away for a bit, and started oxygen and checked her vital signs. Her blood pressure was 80/30 with a faint pulse of 110 and respiratory rate of 10. I was taken aback by what I was experiencing. I was sure she had died, and for more than 15 minutes she did not breathe or have a pulse. It was possible that she had a distant ventricular fibrillation, which reverted back to a normal rhythm when she was shaken repeatedly. Whatever the case, she was conscious now and speaking much clearer as time passed. After one hour, she was still very lethargic; however, she was now speaking full sentences. She asked for a rosary and began to pray. At one point she said, "Thank you, God, for what you showed me. Please help my mom now."

More composed now, Mary and I were listening to Misty attentively. Mary asked her, "Misty, what did God show you?"

Still weak, but remarkably determined to speak, she said, "I was shown the intensity of our spiritual bond could only be released through mutual willingness, and anything contrary could keep my soul from departing the earthly realm. In our case, Mom, your profound sorrow and pain drew me back into my lifeless body. I was already out of my body, and Dad and Mommo and Popo were there. In fact they are still floating above me."

Throughout the next several days, Misty spoke of her out-of-body experience. She knew Mary, Tabetha, and I would like to know more about the next realm. The following is a dialogue between the four of us.

"How did it feel to be of your body?"

"It was so wonderful and peaceful. The one thing I noticed immediately was that I was not feeling an ounce of pain. The next was that I had never felt so at peace and so happy, especially under the circumstances. We were all in total bliss."

Mary: "Are Daddy, Mommo, and Popo still here, honey?"

"Yes, Mom. Daddy, Mommo, and Popo all love you both very much and want you to know they are sitting next to both of you. I can see the light they have now all around both of you. Daddy is above you both."

Tabetha: "Do they have anything to tell us that will make us feel less sad?"

"Yes, Sis. They are so proud of how strong, faithful, hopeful, and God-loving both of you have remained. They want all of you to know, and that includes you, Dr. Lerma, that one should never, ever lose hope that God and all souls are alive in this other world next to yours. It is from your hope that they are able to accomplish their missions."

"Can you ask them to reveal the plan God has for your mother and sister? I just know this would help them cope with so much pain."

"Of course I will. They have told me that they are excited about the plan God has for both of you. You both will be helping so many souls find their way back to God. Mom, you have to believe me when I say that we do not die and that there is a way, way bigger plan where we as an individual or group, with God's guidance, choose a role that will realize a plan that will exceed even the joy and love that are currently felt in the spiritual world. Daddy said that our continued conviction would allow for individual and collective free will to exist for the first time in the eternal existence of God."

Mary: "Honey, are you tired? Do you want to sleep?"

"Mom, I am okay now, especially with the IV fluids Dr. Lerma is giving me and the light that is surrounding my body. I am feeling so much stronger, Mom. Don't worry."

Mary: "Honey, are you going to be leaving soon?"

With that question, Mary, Tabetha, and Misty began crying as the three of them held each other tightly in bed. The three of them looked so beautiful lying in bed together. I closed my eyes and imagined the three of them immersed in the golden, shimmering light Misty spoke of. The girls stopped crying as I began to sense an incredible amount of peace in the room. The hairs on my arms were standing. I remembered that this usually happened when I was around static electricity or in the rooms of patients who were having visions. Was it possible that the spirit's essence was releasing electromagnetic or electrostatic charges? I noticed that the girls' hair was rising at the ends.

I was amazed at Misty's vast improvement. Was she dead when I pronounced her? Misty would be the fifth case. What happened to Misty had occurred four times previously in my hospice career, and each time the patient woke up and explained to their loved ones that their pain and sorrow had pulled them back from a place of peace and love.

Most families understood the possibility of this occurring, so they always remained very respectful of their loved one's final journey. Occasionally, there were those extremely painful cases where the family and patient had lived with grief most of their lives. It was quite understandable to see these families fight to keep their terminally ill loved one alive. Misty told me that these families needed much comfort from God, so one of the ways he provided it was by allowing their pain and sorrow to draw their deceased loved one back to their world and allow him or her to divulge knowledge from the heavenly realm. Of course, the patient had to agree, and most usually did. Misty whispered to her mom that her time was close and she wanted to make sure they would know she was still alive outside of her body and would come back for them really soon.

Mary: "Is there any other way that is less painful to accomplish God's loving plan?"

"Mom, I am told there is no other way to achieve this vast level of infinite freedom and power, but to be born in a fragile complex body and world of two sides, where the human senses can create choices, such as joy and love, or sadness and hatred. Every soul must learn to reconcile these choices through love and forgiveness, so that our free will can have the choice to invite God to live inside of us. It is at this stage that both can experience each other's love, which is and has always been God. It is about that choice that God created us for. When we invite him into our soul, I am told his joy is beyond measure."

Mary: "Did our family choose this level of suffering?"

"Yes, Mom. Our family chose one of the most painful but rewarding ways to save souls and usher in God's plan. Everyone's part is equally important, but some like you and Tabetha continue on Earth to affect a larger part. Mom and Tabetha, don't lose hope. Your part is almost done. Then we can all be together to help others."

"From what part of the body did your soul leave?"

"From my chest region."

"What does your soul look like?"

"Pure light that is made up of our reconciled essence. Dr. Lerma, when humans look at spirits, their mind shapes the essence of light into images that the mind can comprehend what it sees. Similar to the brain, computers work in the same way. They need a certain program to decipher a certain image. Spirits to each other appear as transparent lighted figures."

"How did you handle your uncontrolled physical and emotional pain?"

"The angels or spirits would take me out of my body to wonderful places around the universe."

"Is there life on other planets?"

"Yes. Isn't that wonderful? One day soon, people on our planet will be told. Spiritual leaders on Earth are already working to reveal this. Humans will soon be given the truth about how God created them. I do not recall the exact way, but it will be quite exciting, to say the least."

"Do all spirits feel joyful all the time?"

"Joy is a constant when you are with God; however, there is a subtle sadness for our family and essentially all souls that are not in the heavenly realm. The spirits alongside God never cease from praying for us and helping us along our journey."

"Do other souls feel total sadness and shame?"

"Yes. Those who cannot get past forgiving themselves, so as to understand that God has forgiven us, feel very sad, shameful, regretful, and so forth. These souls are loved very much by God and all of us around God. We try to help them as well, and will never cease. These souls do understand that we want to help them, but they desire to suffer for the sins they were never able to clear before dying. They truly want to make things right, and believe that by suffering this will happen. This part they do not understand. So, many go on and on until they ask for help. The souls I saw had been in this state for more than 6,000 years by Earth time."

"Is every plan for each soul always successful?"

"My dad use to tell me that every play in football is designed to score a touchdown. Yet, the plan to score is usually met with resistance and sometimes one does not score on the first try. So more chances are given and new game plans are tried. Quite the same up here."

"When you were floating in the air, how did you move?"

"By mere thought. There are no limits or restrictions—only the ones you create."

"If your mom and sister continue to never get over their tremendous pain, how does that affect you?"

"If they could try to get over the pain, even with our help, then I would not be emotionally drawn to this world and I could move on without resistance to help God and other souls create ways to draw souls back home."

"Did you see other souls floating around the hospital that were in the hospice wing?"

"Yes. I saw the man next door. He had passed earlier that morning and his family had not arrived. He was really sad. The angels were calling him and were telling him they would be fine, as would he. Still, he would not go with the angels until he was given closure. He is so drawn to the nurses who were taking care of him, because of their unconditional love for him. I saw you walk in with the nurses and pray with him."

"Is that right, Misty? Did you really see us from your room?"

"Yes, I did. As spirits all matter is transparent, so I could see through the walls."

His son finally came and told him how much he had loved him and then kissed him on his forehead. The nurses and I then prayed with the son. Right after we prayed, the television turned on by itself and the son heard the words *thank you*. He was so excited believing his dad had spoken to him and turned the TV on. He told me his dad had always said he would leave him a sign from the other world.

"You know something, Dr. Lerma. Souls on Earth have so much more power to affect other souls in a good way. Don't forget that."

"Did you see the tunnel of light others claim to see?"

"Not this time, but I have seen it here in the hospice unit. I saw the tunnel of light where others who died. It's really bright and so beautiful."

When my dad died a year before in August 2007, he said when you look at everything as a spirit, everything is extremely bright. He told me a few hours before his death that he was beginning to float out of his body and he could then see my aura and soul. He described my aura as golden bright and my soul as a beautiful bright ocean blue with rays of light emanating toward him. I told him it was because that was my love for him.

"Do you see my dad, Misty?"

"I'm sorry, but no, Dr. Lerma. Because I'm sure your family believes strongly in God and were willing to let him go peacefully, he is probably helping others, but not far away. You would be so surprised to know how close heaven really is, Dr. Lerma."

"When you were out of your body when I pronounced you dead, did you feel a tugging to a higher level?"

"No. Remember it's all by choice up there as it is down here. A soul may choose to stay on the earthly plane of existence or to move forward."

"Why do some choose to stay here?"

"They are lost and looking for their families. Many of these people die suddenly, usually accidents or murders, and did not have a chance to say goodbye, live a decent life, say I'm sorry, or were left with complete and utter anger as they were dying. They are looking for vengeance."

"Are these souls that are looking for vengeance a form of evil?"

"They are just filled with the dark side of their essence. This is the side within our minds that one has to locate, understand, and then release while on earth. It is so much harder to accomplish this in the spirit world. A lack of knowledge of the other side and faith are the two things that allow one to fully learn a lesson. In the next realm, knowledge is fully available and, because one knows God exists, faith is used differently. These dark souls live off of another's energy. They cannot use the energy from God to survive because of opposite polarities. I guess you can say these are ghosts, evil spirits lurking the earth, and cosmos for energy to survive—very much like vampires. To protect oneself from these entities, one must not invite them in your home or soul by speaking to them. It is very dangerous. Yet, remember that believing in the god that created this dark soul will protect you. Pray for him to find peace and forgiveness and for God and his angels to guide him to another place away from his people on Earth. Remember that the God of all things loves all things equally and will never cease from helping his lost sheep find there way back home."

"Are you going to be healed, Misty?"

"No, Dr. Lerma. I am only here for a few more days—just enough time to allow my mother and sister find peace and closure. This time, my mom and my sister will let me go. The dreams and visions my mom will have for the rest of her life will continue to comfort her beyond measure. My sister will also have experiences, but not to the extent of my mom, as Tabetha is much stronger."

"What visions will your mother and sister have?"

"Tomorrow night they will see Daddy and Mommo and Popo while sleeping in my room. They will talk to them briefly to let them know I will be fine and that they would always be next to them."

"I am so happy for your mom and sister, and ecstatic that you will be pain free, healed, and next to your family in heaven. Are there spirits around us now?"

"Dr. Lerma, they are always around. Here, right now, there are four angels along with my daddy and grandparents. My family is in bliss because the family is all together again. By the way, they are sitting on the opposite side of the bed from you, and are smiling at you and want to thank you for helping my body and my family. Now, the angels are each standing at the different corners of the room. They are transparent and in a protective-type stance, but very loving. They are quite large, about 8 to 10 feet, wearing maroon and golden silk-like flowing garments."

"Why don't we all see angels or spirits like you do right now?"

"One must be in a very relaxed state and have the right chemicals in the brain to give one the ability. You can see them, Dr. Lerma, but why would that matter? One should work on discernment and intuition, which is a form of telepathy. This is where we find the truth. It's what they say that's important, not what they look like. If you need to see them, they will appear. Not seeing them is often a sign that one's earthy journey is not as distressing. That's not to mean that one is not worthy. Angels and souls in this realm do not have a physical body with vocal cords."

"How should one prepare for his or her journey back home?"

"By listening to our intuition, which tells us what is right and wrong and connects us to our Creator. Through this understanding, one needs to find self-forgiveness and self-love through reconciliation, at which point God will manifest himself within each and every soul for eternity."

"Can we experience heaven on Earth?"

"Absolutely! What do you think Jesus meant when he said, 'Where two or more are gathered in my name, there I am in their midst.' Jesus is pure love, which is heaven. To experience a heavenly type life, one has to accept that Jesus forgave all our sins, past, present, and future. Many believe this is too easy and feel they need to suffer before accepting God. This way of thinking is created by the ego, which is self-defeating and self-serving with the ultimate consequence of separation from God. One cannot be judge and jury, if you will, and believe this self-conviction will release us from our guilt and sins, and get us into the heavenly realm. If one chooses to suffer after we die, instead of accepting Jesus' sacrifice for us, then we will be suffering for eternity.

"Our ego will never release us from this guilt-based way of thinking. That is why it is extremely important to understand what the ego is, how it works to separate us from God and others, and how to allow our God spirit to blossom. Bottom line: Reconciliation of the spirit and the ego with God early in our lives, will allow one to live a Godly life with heavenly powers while on Earth. It's really pretty easy if one remains true to Jesus. He wants to be our best friend and give us eternal life without pain and suffering. I am tiring now, Dr. Lerma. Could we talk tomorrow?"

"Sure thing, Misty. Thank you and God for all you have taught me and for reminding about love and forgiveness. Sleep with the angels, Misty."

"You too, Dr. Lerma."

While on my patient rounds early the next morning, I saw Mary sitting on the bench outside Misty's room, looking vibrant. She was smiling and gleaming with joy, and I could tell she was anxious to talk with me. I walked toward her and sat on the beautiful, 18th-century wooden bench. As I sat on the heirloom, it reminded me of the loving family that had donated it. Their 4-year-old son had died from leukemia in the same room that Misty was currently in. He never complained of pain. His mother and father placed the bench in front of his room, so the angels he saw in the room would have a place to sit. I quickly brushed away the tears and asked Mary how she was doing. I am so thankful that God allowed her to come back to teach us and comfort us.

Mary commented, "Dr. Lerma, I apologize for the way I shook my daughter after she was dead. I know I brought her back, but now I am ready to let her go. While both of you talked yesterday afternoon, I fell asleep and dreamed about Misty in heaven with her father and my parents. They looked so happy. They turned to acknowledge my presence and smiled. I told them all I loved them very much, and wanted to do what God felt was best. Without moving their mouths, I clearly heard them tell me not to worry, because God, the angels, and the four of them would always be close by to help and would be back soon to welcome me and Tabetha back home. Then the dream was over and I was left with the odor of roses on my pillow. Red roses are my favorite."

"Have you seen Misty this morning?" I asked Mary.

"Yes. I woke up early and slipped into her bed next to her. She was no longer conscious, and her breathing was slow and shallow. I knew she was leaving, so I held her so, so tight, until she breathed her last breath and slowly and calmly released it. I saw a tear roll down her cheek. She had left this world, and her body, with the most beautiful smile of her life. I knew she had finally seen the glory of God. With that one thought, my entire being was filled with God's glory, and then I saw the brightest flash of light coming from the foot of her bed. I saw God's glory, Dr. Lerma!"

9 A True Miraculous Healing

For I will restore health unto thee, and will heal thee of thy wounds, saith the lord…
—Jeremiah 30:17

Intuitively drawn toward the entrance to her bedroom, Maggie saw a magnificent and radiant creature floating on glowing white mist almost 2 feet above the floor. Entranced by the entity's ethereal beauty, Maggie opened her heart and invited her to enter. Within seconds, the angel, whose name was Magdalene, effortlessly glided across the doorway and toward the right side of her bed. The shimmering light that once surrounded Magdalene was now permeating Maggie's disease-ravaged body and the entire bedroom. Maggie's heart was racing from the mere excitement of being in the midst of a divine being. She looked up at the angel with her beautifully crooked smile, and was instantly captivated by the depth of wisdom in her eyes. As their eyes locked onto each other, Maggie felt hypnotized by the depth of wisdom within her alluring blue eyes. What Maggie saw next filled her with a great sense of hope, along with an outlying feeling of apprehension. "Dr. Lerma, it was as clear as day. I saw myself helping many people at the end of my life, with an emphasis on two children who had been severely injured. I appeared to be much healthier-looking, and more vibrant. I saw myself praying for people who were suffering. I could see and feel a warm, bright light radiate from my hands and envelop all those souls who I was praying for. Magdalene told me that God used me as his vessel to heal these people. Two young children remained and, for whatever reason, I was not allowed to touch them; however, I felt that the three of us would play an integral role in each other's healing. Was it possible that God was going to heal me so that I could live the rest of my life helping and healing others? Could this really be a divine message relaying that others, along with myself, would be healed? Or was I merely hallucinating? What was I supposed to do, Dr. Lerma?"

"Maggie, what I can tell you is that you are definitely not in a delirious state, hallucinating, or having a lucid dream. Remember when I walked into the room and walked past the angel."

"Yes. I asked you to move because you were standing in front of Magdalene. When you moved, I was able to see her clearly again."

"*Maggie, since you could not see the angel when I stood in front of her, this clearly tells me that the vision is in the physical world. It is not being projected into your mind, similar to lucid dreaming or hallucinations.*"

"So, Dr. Lerma, does that mean that I am actually seeing something in our world that you cannot see?"

"*Until I have a better scientific explanation, I would tend to agree with you. Maggie, it appears you have the ability to visualize images and things in our world, which, for some unknown reason, another human cannot see. I suspect it might have something to do with your advanced disease process that somehow stimulates the production of new neurotransmitters, such as Dimethyltryptamine (DMT), that trigger part(s) of the brain previously untapped, to be activated. Just before my father passed away, he explained that, when God created the dynamics of our brain, he gifted us with super-senses, which would exceed our five senses. He said the human brain had so many abilities that had not been harnessed. Some were on the verge of evolving into our species, and others were hundreds to thousands of years away.*

"*My dad explained that humans were in the process of becoming aware of their sixth sense, which encompasses telepathy, clairvoyance, precognition, and intuitive strengths, and even the seventh, which deals with a super-visual sense, such as remote viewing, which the CIA continues to research. In other words, it is an ability to see the spiritual world or physical world from a distance. The eighth, ninth, and 10th senses are close to evolving into our material world.*

He said they had to do with dematerialization of the human body, communication with the ethereal world, connection with the energy that connects everything and everyone, and being able to change the course of atmospheric events, such as hurricanes, tornadoes, and earthquakes, so as to help our fellow man. Politics and religion as we know then will evolve to bring about unification of the human race, instead of being divisive."

Maggie felt more at ease then, knowing that she might actually be seeing something beautiful and loving in her room and not in her mind.

As Maggie and I sat contemplating the possibilities of her visions and opening our hearts to God's will, she knew healing would occur, but not hers. She understood that the power to heal was momentary, and would only be given to someone who was suffering and wanted to keep suffering willfully and joyfully. In doing so, others would experience the entire benefit of the healing process. Maggie told me that willful suffering weakens the dark side, and allows for complete experience of God's powers, including that of healing. "Dr. Lerma, suffering will one day rid us completely of our sinful nature and ego. I appreciate suffering for this reason. Whether we want to believe it or not, we are all doing our parts to permanently extinquish our weaknesses and dark and egoistic ways."

Blissfully, Maggie welcomed the physical and emotional suffering that accompanied her cancer, so that she would follow God's will of healing those people he brought to her, along with the two young children she had seen in her vision.

With great faith, Maggie and I waited for the sign that would let us know that she was ready to heal the afflicted. Two weeks had passed since her vision and message, and there was no sign that Maggie was endowed with the power of healing. Indeed, this was a difficult time, as it would test our patience and faith. She continued to decline physically during the next two to four weeks. Her pain was spreading, as the cancer grew in her bones, but her symptoms of nausea, vomiting, and dehydration were kept at bay with intravenous medications. Maggie and I still trusted that the angel was correct, and we waited with bated breath.

Three weeks after her initial visit and spiritual experience, once again Maggie began to communicate with the glorious entity. Maggie had the nurses call me to tell me that it was happening. Exhausted from running up the stairs, I sighed as I entered Maggie's room. "I am seeing that beautiful being again, Dr. Lerma."

Slightly confused from the morphine, Maggie could not decide who the entity was. At times, what Maggie was saying was really funny. I am always amazed at the angel's ability to make my patients laugh. In doing so, they've always made me laugh. Experiencing this always made me feel very peaceful and hopeful. "Is that entity my deceased mother? Nope. Her hair never looked that good. Is it my husband, Joey? I don't think so. He never wore long clean robes, and the last time I saw him with long hair was when he dressed up for Halloween. Joey, is that you? If that's not you, then who are you?"

Maggie's cognition quickly cleared up, and she went on to say that the angel finally introduced herself as Magdalene. In what seemed to be hours, yet was in actuality only a few seconds, Magdalene told Maggie that her time on earth was coming to an end and she would be coming back daily to help with her physical pain as well as her emotional and spiritual healing. Magdalene and Maggie looked at each other and looked into each other's eyes again. Magdalene replayed the vision of Maggie praying and healing many others, including the two children. Maggie, now quite weak, once again looked up and showed her crooked smile. She said that Magdalene continued to return daily, usually in the morning, at which time she would let her know who was coming to visit and what issues needed to be resolved, if at all possible.

The number of angels increased as her time on Earth was coming to an end. The last week before her transition, she said there were more than 20 light beings floating around the corners of her bedroom and behind anyone that was in the room. They were now allowed to stay with her 24 hours a day, as they were to provide comfort from her escalating physical and emotional pain. Maggie's body was now exhibiting signs of intense pain, yet she stoically refused any additional pain medication. It was during this period of selfless suffering that Maggie was graced with the gift of healing.

Maggie remained exuberant and exhilarated as her physical condition worsened, and she attributed this joyful attitude to a disconnect of her nervous system. "Dr. Lerma, I believe that connecting with the angels and communicating with them removes me from the pain that my body is mounting. As long as I keep fastened to the spiritual world, I will not sense any level of discomfort. Dr. Lerma, please let people know that staying connected to God, either by thinking about him, talking with him, talking to others about him, sharing his works in your life to others, and always involving him in everything you do, or plan to do or say, will remove any distress in their life. This may be difficult at first, but in a short period of time one will see the results."

Many of my patients had tried to explain this process, but until then, I did understand the mechanism. It made so much sense.

I could sense the loving energy in her room, as did all the nurses. Visitors and medical staff began to notice that merely walking into her room would result in the alleviation and often permanent removal of their chronic pains and emotional distress. Word spread around the hospital of Maggie's abilities to abolish one's pain, and soon workers were visiting and being healed through Maggie's loving touch, and other patients were wheeled from other rooms, at her request, and were healed from several types of pain. My own migraines would spontaneously remit after Maggie touched my forehead. I had heard of cancer patients who were able to reduce their doses of morphine and methadone by 90 percent and remain almost pain-free for weeks through means of meditation, but to heal others and not thyself was beyond comprehension. Maggie was meditating, and what pain was relieved was not for herself, but for everyone else in her presence.

Several days after Maggie's second vision of Magdalene, a 14-year-old boy named Billy and his 10-year-old sister, Jodie, had been admitted in critical condition for what appeared to be a gruesome and inconceivable act of revenge by their stepfather. Billy and Jodie were drenched in gasoline and then set on fire in the backyard of their home. Shortly after he threw a lit match on Billy and Jodie, the next-door neighbor saw the fireball and heard the screaming. She immediately ran toward them, jumped the fence, picked them both up while on fire, and jumped into the pool. In the end, Billy and Jodie had more than 80 percent of their little bodies burned. Miraculously, their faces, heads, necks, and hands were not injured, and the woman who saved them had no evidence of any significant burn marks.

The night they were admitted, the children could be heard crying from the horrific pain. Not even the high dose of intravenous morphine was effective. The nurse caring for the children, Stacey, had visited Maggie earlier that day with the hope of being healed from a 10-year battle with anxiety and depression. As she sat next to Maggie and took hold of her hands, Maggie immediately sensed her pain, and then turned almost 180 degrees toward the right corner of the room, as if listening to an unseen force. Because her depression stemmed from her concern for her daughter, the spiritual beings wanted Stacey to know that her daughter, Missy, was helping so many from heaven and not to worry about her.

With a peaceful look and with tears in her eyes, Stacey hugged Maggie and thanked her profusely. I had never seen a person with major depression shift so rapidly to the polar opposite. "Stacey, God and your daughter want you to be comforted and healed from your depression and anxiety, because they love you. You do not owe them anything, Stacey. Your joy is enough. Don't ever forget that your daughter, along with so many other departed daughters, sons, and relatives, are alive and well in heaven. You will see her soon. No need to rush. God wants you to enjoy whatever years you have left on this planet, and use them to help yourself get closer to God, and then help others."

Maggie quickly turned to Stacey's right, and intently listened and nodded her head. She then turned to Stacey and told her what she was told. "Be happy, Mom. Just be happy. By being happy, you will be able to see God in everything. You will see me, too. That's all God wants. I love you, Mommy. I am so proud of you."

There was not a dry eye in the room, nor enough Kleenex, after we heard Missy's words. I was in total awe of the love that Maggie imparted on us. Almost instantly, Stacy's anxiety and depression changed to that of total joy, peace, and unconditional love. As she hugged Maggie to thank her, she caught a glimpse of her daughter float upward and through the ceiling. Stacey told me later that she clearly heard her daughter say, "I am always with you, Mommy, and you will see me again real soon."

Maggie was now growing weaker by the day, but she insisted on healing people from their pain until her last breath. When she heard the horrific and sad story of the two burned children, she asked me if I would allow her to be placed on a gurney and taken to their room. Without delay, I had the nurses help me place Maggie's fragile body on the gurney. She cried and cried when she finally laid eyes on the children, as she felt their anguish. The children's mother had already heard about her healing powers, and was quite anxious to have Maggie touch her children. When she saw Maggie, she reached out in desperation, and pleaded with her to heal her children. Because the children were in isolation to protect them from infections, I helped place the appropriate attire on Maggie and pushed the gurney into their room. With tears rolling down Billy and Jodie's faces, Maggie told them to open their eyes fully and look up toward the right side of their bed. The children eagerly followed her commands and looked up and to their right. Before they could fully open their eyes, I saw the children begin to smile. They were no longer crying. In fact, it looked like they were in a euphoric trance. Billy and Jodie began to talk, but without emitting any type of vocal sound. Only Maggie and the children were involved in the conversation.

Within 10 minutes, the children sat back in bed, closed their now-peaceful eyes, wiped their tears with the part of their hands that were not burned or wrapped in gauze, and fell asleep. It was simply mind-boggling. Why was this beautiful story not on CNN, Fox, CBS, or even Nancy Grace? It is always the fear-based stories full of condemnation and judgment that make the news. Rarely, if ever, does one hear about forgiveness, random acts of kindness, and visions of God and his angels. This was definitely an example of where our society was run by the self-serving, hateful and non-forgiving ego.

At that time, Maggie asked to go back to her room. She needed to come back a few more times to make sure the children were free of their emotional and physical pain, and to pray for the healing of their wounds. I obliged Maggie for four more days, and on the fifth day Maggie had an awesome vision. Her parents, along with Missy, Magdalene, and an immense bright, white light, were now at the foot of her bed. The light began to take the shape of a tunnel, which surfaced from the space between the foot of the bed and the wall. The tunnel was some-where between 4 and 5 feet in length and 6 feet wide. Maggie commented that the sum of the angelic spirits in the room was now more than 30 and they were all lifting their hands toward the light, as in reverence. Maggie saw a figure walking out of the lighted passage, which began to shimmer from white, to blue, to gold. "Despite the great force of the light, it did not hurt my eyes, nor did I need to squint. In fact, the brighter it got, the better I saw, heard, and felt. It penetrated every fiber of my being, as well as every element, molecule, and atom around the room. This energy certainly brought out the best in me."

Maggie felt exhilarated, joyful, peaceful, and ecstatic. What Maggie saw next was apparently beyond magnificent. "Dr. Lerma, I saw a golden figure at the foot of her bed, and then felt someone cleansing my feet and loving me beyond all understanding. All I could see at the foot of the bed was a brilliant, golden light, with no obvious shape. I did hear a loving voice emanating from the light, telling me that he was ready to take me home, but only after I carried his healing power to Billy and Jodie one more time.

'After you do that Maggie, I will return for you,' the voice from the light remarked. 'Pray for the stepfather and remind the children to forgive him as well, and to pray that he finds love and forgiveness.'"

Maggie was taken to visit the children the next day, and once again the children's pain was lifted. In fact, only five days into their hospital stay, their temperatures returned to normal, and they were eating 100 percent of their meals. Their remaining pain was controlled solely with Tylenol. This was simply astounding. That evening, Maggie fell into a coma and, with a smile from ear to ear, she took her last breath on Earth and her first breath in heaven.

Doctor's Notes

Three months later, I visited the children in a rehabilitation hospital, and the third-degree burns were healing without the

the usual scars. In fact, most of the burns healed without necessity for skin grafts. Maggie had indeed placed her healing hands on the children and transferred the healing power of God—the same God that humbly washed her feet in humility. Billy and Jodie still talk about the angels and Maggie, telling their mother that they visit quite frequently.

10 Prophesy and the Holy Land

In the last days, "God says, 'I will pour my spirit on all people. Your son's and daughters will prophesy. Your young men will see visions. And your old men will dream dreams...and everyone who calls on my name will be saved.'"

—Acts 2:17

It had been a truly emotional and challenging day for me, as three beautiful, loving children between the ages of 7 and 14 had passed away. They had been sages like the rest of my patients, and, similar to so many other children, they were encircled with more than 30 divine angels and several animals, of which the cats, dogs, dolphins, and giraffes were their favorites. With a smile from ear to ear, Jimmy, the 7 year old, told me that morning he was "going to be getting on the giraffe, holding on real tight, because the angels are taking me to play with the dolphins and the other children." I had heard this same story over and over from most of my young patients, but Jimmy would say something so mind-boggling and surreal that I had to pinch myself to make certain I was not dreaming.

In what would be Jimmy's last words to me, he looked at me and told me, "Someone here wants me to tell you hello." Understanding that one should always make an attempt at entertaining a serious conversation with a patient, I asked Jimmy who the message was from. "It's from a little boy that you helped, like me. His name is Matthew." Immediately, I felt the most magnificent rush of cool air permeate my very essence. I now had the biggest smile. Two of us in the room had smiles from ear to ear. *"Could you ask him how he is doing?"*

I had not even finished my sentence when Jimmy responded with the answers, as though they were reading my thoughts. I was bewildered. "He is feeling great and he wants me to tell you he is going to take me to ride the dolphins. He wants me to tell you goodbye and will see you later."

Was it possible that this was Matthew, the 9-year-old patient I had cared for two years before? There is no way that Jimmy could have known about Matthew's story, as he was in a different hospice facility and I had not mentioned the story to the new nurses or the family. In addition, my first book had not been released. I hugged Jimmy, and he hugged me back. As I pulled back, I looked into his eyes and he into mine, and I knew at that moment that he was telling me the truth. What I saw in his eyes was wonderfully familiar. It was as though I could see the shimmering reflection of the heavenly realm with Matthew riding on the back of a dolphin. This picture is seared forever in my memory and soul, and for that I will be forever grateful to Jimmy, Matthew, and God's angels.

The day was almost over, and I entered the hospice family room to relax for a moment before my next patient arrived. As I went to sit on the chair that had comforted thousands of family members, I was startled by a loud banging sound. It seemed to be coming from the windows, which in and of themselves were astonishing. They were 12-foot-high, old English windows with ivy-covered lattice that spanned the entire length of the ornate windows. As I walked gently across the wooden planks of this old English Mansion, I noticed the oak trees and the manicured hedges swaying intensely. It was late October, and I was quickly reminded that this forceful wind was the cold front we had been expecting all day. I felt a sudden cold draft from small cracks on the windows, so I started a fire. I located the firewood and asked the nurse to bring me a lighter and a hot cup of cocoa. With the fire lit, and my cocoa on the lamp table next to the chair, I sank into the chair, turned on the television to watch the world news, and soon found myself falling asleep.

Syriana, my next young patient with terminal cancer, was running late because of the gale-force winds and plummeting temperatures. With my eyes closed, I found myself listening to the seemingly unending media reports of deaths around the world, especially in the Middle East. I was disgusted at the hundreds of senseless killings. Here I was in a beautifully refurbished mansion turned hospice, comforting people as they died, and a few thousand miles to my east were healthy women, men, and children being massacred in the name of God. Was this the same God that my young patients were being comforted by? If so, how could he allow the infliction of horrific pain to certain children and families, and at the same time comfort and love children and families across the world?

I was deeply conflicted. I was so accustomed to experiencing His acts of unconditional love and forgiveness that he imparted not only on those who had led loving lives, but also for those who did not. What was going on? Was God not the way I had envisioned in totality? If God was not responsible, then where was he?

I remember at that moment one of the profound messages Matthew had left me with regard to suffering and the darkness of the world.

"Dr. Lerma, Jesus can do anything he wants, including the ability to stop wars and killing and even destroy our world. He is not on a throne somewhere like we think he is. He is within all of us and, as such, he relies on us to stop these atrocities, as well as hunger, hatred, poverty, and so forth. He helps those who help themselves, and who desire in their heart and soul to make a change. The act of helping our fellow man, no matter from what culture, race, gender, or religion, is the form of willful suffering that God responds to, and boy does he respond.

Essentially, Jesus, who lives within us, knows our heart and our desires, and, if one has a strong desire to help another, you do not even have to ask him verbally, as he knows our will at the point we conceived it before it entered our brain. Now, for those who choose to keep killing, there is not much he can do, unless he hears the prayers of the people of the world to help the true victims. Now, if a soul chooses to die in a certain circumstance, or suffer for others, like I did in order to save my mom and sisters from themselves, no amount of prayer can change their free-will. It is all very complicated, especially with free will in the mix. Bottom line: Just pray from you heart and soul that God's will will be done. God's will is always prefect!"

I recalled how other patients had spoken about the negative impact the media has on our souls. Apparently, by watching the news I was exposing my soul to the traumatic reality of the world, which in turn would awaken my higher spirit, usually leading one to hope that these unspeakable crimes ended. However, they would also continue watching how pure darkness would place one's soul at risk to self-separate from our Creator. How, you ask? By questioning God. So, I turned off the television and opened the medical chart of Syriana. Here was another casualty of cancer, and at such a young age. She was only 16 years old, and was now sentenced to die from a rare form of bone cancer, which her oncologist related to exposure to plutonium-cased shells. How did this innocent girl get exposed to these irradiated casings. As I turned the pages of Syriana's medical chart, the answers were clear and succinct and beyond comprehension. The story of her life began to unravel. Syriana had been born in Lebanon to a very wealthy God-loving Muslim family. Her father, who was in the oil business, would travel often to the United States with his family, and they were placed in the best schools in Lebanon, Spain, and England. However, through the course of their travels, Syriana and her two siblings were exposed to radioactive bombsites and shell casings. Many of the children she played with became quite ill and were diagnosed with many forms of leukemia and cancer.

One evening, during Ramadan, Syriana's family was finishing their evening prayers and getting ready to eat. Her 45-year-old mother and father, 14-year-old sister, 12-year-old brother, and she, now 15 years old, sat at the table and began praying. All of a sudden, their father screamed to get under the table. They all held hands and closed their eyes. Syriana recalls vividly at that moment that just before a missile exploded, they were all startled by the brightest white light she had ever seen. She remembers looking at the faces of her family, and instead of seeing intense fright she saw them smiling and looking up toward the tunnel of light. Syriana said it was beautifully white and inviting and covering all of them. Time and space seemed to have slowed down.

"We then heard a popping sound, after which our individual spirits were able to escape our motionless bodies. Our spirits floated from the bottom of the table. In fact we floated right through the table. It felt so cool to do so. We were all floating, transparent, light beings now moving toward the tunnel of the whitest light I had ever seen. My family and I were immediately drawn by the love and joy that radiated from the tunnel along with the appearance of several transparent beings like ourselves. As we walked from the interior of the light tunnel toward us, we all recognized them to be our family and friends. It was Grandma, Grandpa, and many of my friends who had either been killed or who had died recently from cancer. Their faces were so young and peaceful-looking, and their robes or vestments were whiter than the whitest snow."

Through telepathy, they spoke to all of us collectively and explained that God had allowed time to stop to allow for separation from their physical body in an attempt to keep them from the pain of the missile. One of the angels explained that not all of them would be entering the light this time. "Only Mom, your brother, and sister are to enter the light. Your father and you, Syriana, will remain on Earth to accomplish the loving lessons God and both of you agreed upon a long, long time ago. God is so proud of all of you and will never abandon you. Your father and you will need to go back to finish your divine design, which will not only bring your souls back to the Creator, but will also draw back countless numbers of souls. The key is to open your heart to the final truth that will set you free. Your mother and siblings have accepted the truth and now are being accepted in the Kingdom of God."

Syriana asked, "Why can't you tell me what the truth is? I thought that we had had learned and followed the teachings of the Qur'an?" The angel told Syriana that there was nothing to worry about: "You will see the truth soon, but will be unaware what you are seeing is the One Truth. The One Truth will find you and you will know it was inside you all along. This One Truth needs to be accepted by all in this world, so you are not alone."

Just before her mother left, she told her husband and Syriana to forgive those who killed them and, above all, to remember to open their hearts to the One Truth. The One Truth we have thought all of our lives was a lie.

"Okay, Mom. I will find it and accept it."

As her mother, siblings, grandparents, friends, and angels floated into the tunnel of white light, the frozen frame began to slowly move forward along with their free-floating spirits.

"Within a second, Dad and I were back in our bodies and under the table, but with rocks and stones all around us. The missile hit next to our home along with several others. My dad and I were grasping each other's hands tightly with an overwhelming feeling of joy and unconditional love. As I saw a light flicker in the distance, I briefly thought my mom was coming back for us, but, as it got closer, I realized it was something more earthly. The beams were coming from flashlights. It was the police and firemen, who were looking for survivors. I remember how these lights were much dimmer, and yet my eyes were more sensitive, as opposed to the bright white light from the tunnel of heaven. The police finally pulled us out of the rubble, and, although we had several broken bones and organ injuries, miraculously we had no head or spinal cord injuries. One of the men pulling me out made a comment that I was in shock, because I was inappropriately giggling and smiling. I was so joyful because of having been immersed in the light of God."

Both recoveries were daunting, but after six months they were released from the hospital. Syriana and her father were so depressed, traumatized, and angry, even though they had seen their family enter the light. Their lives were turned upside-down, but the worst, as Syriana put it, was their internal spiritual conflict. More than six months had passed, and Syriana and her father could not find forgiveness for the killers, and even themselves, for thinking this way.

Throughout the next few weeks, Syriana began to improve mentally and spiritually, but her father continued to fester in his anger and retribution. He did not want to influence his daughter any further, so he gave her most of his fortune and sent her to live with his sisters in the West Bank of the Jordan River. Her father had turned crazed and obsessed by using his money to hire officials to investigate the bombing.

Syriana revealed that her father called her one night, and, while crying over the phone, he saw the tunnel of light, from which came a man with a beard and long crimson robe. This man had points of light radiating from his hands, feet, chest, and forehead. Syriana said that all she heard was, "My Lord. It is you. I am so sorry. Please forgive me. I love you, Syriana. I will be back real soon for you. Your mother was right. The One Truth is not new. It has always been in us. You will see. I love you."

He hung up, and Syriana was unable to get through to him.

The next day, Syriana was told that her father had passed away the previous night in his sleep. Syriana cried a few tears, as she knew her time was close. She too had been feeling ill, and had felt she would die soon. Within weeks, Syriana was diagnosed with osteosarcoma, or bone cancer, and it had spread throughout her body. One of her aunts was an internal medicine physician, and felt she would die in Palestine, as their oncology treatment was virtually nonexistent. Syriana's aunt was able to get her an appointment with an oncologist friend of hers in Israel. He ended up evaluating Syriana, but her cancer was so advanced that he believed the only option was to attempt experimental drugs, located at Sloan Kettering or MD Anderson; both were in the United States. This was not a problem, because Syriana had an open visa and money. The oncologist said that her osteosarcoma was uncommon, but in recent years he had seen large numbers of children not only with osteosarcoma, but many rare leukemias. It was later found that these children had been exposed to low levels of radiation for long periods, likely from plutonium-cased shells. Syriana's father had a brother in the United States who was a physician, andn after he was told about her illness, he called several of his friends in Houston, and within one week she was accepted to MD Anderson. Her visa was obtained shortly thereafter, and she headed for MD Anderson Hospital in Houston, Texas.

As I skipped to the psychosocial portion of her medical chart, I came across a psychiatrist's consulting notes. Evidently, the oncologist asked the psychiatrist to address her delirium, which included visual, auditory, and tactile hallucinations. The physician quickly discounted the visions of Jesus and her parents, brother, and sisters as mere chemically induced hallucinations. Nowhere in the chart was there an in-depth description about the visions other than who she saw. Despite a grueling four-month experimental trial of chemotherapy, along with intense radiation, the cancer cells, seemingly unaffected, metastasized to the majority of her bones as well as vital organs. Her oncologist wrote in his last progress note:

"Like the large numbers of children and teenagers I have treated, Syriana has recently shown a strong desire to live. Yet, unlike all of my patients past and present, Syriana's explanation was vastly different and beyond comprehension. She recently told me that she did not want to die, but to live, only if she could live with her cancer. Syriana understood the visions of her deceased family to be a gift from God via the disease process. At any other time, I would have related these so-called 'visions' to be hallucinations from her toxemia and chemotherapeutic agents; however, because she was not delirious or confused, it had to be a type of conversion coping mechanism in response to her past and present trauma. Clearly, Syriana had been through so much stress and loss. Syriana's experiences could also be the non-linear terminal hallucinations type that many patients have experienced just before their death. However, her prognosis was not impending. Either way, with her cancer growing exponentially, it was not prudent and necessary to discontinue her experimental treatments at this time, and pursue palliative measures."

Her oncologist called me the following day and explained Syriana's reaction to her prognosis of one to three months. "Dr. Lerma, I had not even finished the sentence when she took my hand and told me not to worry, and then thanked me profusely. I had never seen her this happy. She was in sheer euphoria. She told me she understood if I thought she was crazy for reacting this way, but she hoped I understood that her joy came from knowing that she would continue to have visions of her family and soon be walking through the light with them and many, many angels. Having heard you speak at a conference about the types of visions, beings, and locations of appearances, I thought you would appreciate knowing that during her exuberance, she looked toward the foot of the bed, sat up, raised her arms, as in praise, and said, 'Thank you, my Lord. You are The One Truth and Lord of all and I love you so, so much!'"

With the whistling sound of our first cold front making its way around the three-story hospice facility, and the crackling sounds of the wood giving way to hot flames, I closed Syriana's chart, snuggled into the leather chair, and fell asleep. I entered REM sleep immediately, and was dreaming of Syriana and myself, watching one of my favorite episodes of *Seinfeld* about the Soup Nazi. Syriana and I were laughing so hard. Within the hour, the nurse woke me to tell me that Syriana was 10 minutes away. As I awoke, I was still feeling so invigorated from the humorous dream that I still had a grin from ear to ear. Somehow I felt that I was already introduced to Syriana's jovial and loving spirit, and she was foreshadowing a relationship of laughter, joy, and deep conversations. I was truly excited about meeting this passionate, loving, and witty soul. I stood up and contently walked to the physician on-call room to freshen up, after which I headed to meet Syriana.

As I walked into Syriana's room, I felt a strong positive energy that I knew was exuding from her cheerful essence. As I turned to face her, I could not believe my eyes. Lying on the oversized hospital bed was a small girl who was emaciated. I lost my smile for a moment until I heard the most beautiful and peaceful-sounding voice coming from the severely diseased body. "Oh now, come on, Dr. Lerma, don't be sad for me. Didn't you hear that my responses and actions are opposite of the average human? Now, if I had a healthy-looking body, I would certainly be sad and dejected. So, I am overly thin—okay, I'm sickly thin. That just means that I am really, really happy. In fact, I am feeling exhilarated right now."

I could not help but smile and laugh. "That's better, Doctor. That's a great smile."

"Syriana, I am sorry, I did not mean to look sad. In all honesty, I am really excited and honored to be part of your awesome spiritual journey. I want you to be part of my journey as well. By any chance, do you like the TV program Seinfeld?"

Syriana replied, "I actually started to watch it a few months ago, along with *Everybody Loves Raymond*, and now I look forward to watching them before I go to sleep. Why do you ask?"

I told her they were also my favorites and maybe sometime we could watch them together and laugh. This was uncanny, wondering whether the dream I had earlier was merely telepathy or coincidence.

Syriana said, "Your dream was just a precursor to things to come."

I stepped out to let the nurses finish their assessment and to make her comfortable. Meanwhile, I went to the family room to speak to Syriana's uncle. He was a hematologist and had been living in Dallas, Texas, for the previous 15 years. He told me that after the bombing that killed most of his brother's family, he was contacted by his brother asking him to make sure he would watch out for Syriana.

Syriana's uncle told me that Syriana has been a very special girl since birth. She had certain abilities to foresee the future, and several times the family, through Syriana's prophetic messages, was able to avert certain death. Somehow, she was unable to foresee the danger that awaited her family with this last bomb.

The doctor went on to describe how she would obtain these messages. He said that one day while the entire family was visiting a mosque in East Jerusalem, they could not find her for several hours. She returned to the mosque after two hours, telling her mother that a Jewish man with a long beard and beautiful blue eyes took her around the Holy Land, and explained the history of the Christian, Jewish, and Muslim faiths. He told her that they all had the same God and would return to the same God eventually. Everyone moves forward, no matter what, she was told. Granted, some go through a more intense and longer path of learning to love and forgive. Syriana said that this man told her about the despicable crimes that had occurred and would continue occurring here until a radical change occurred in consciousness. That time was out there, but unknown. Syriana said that when she asked him if her family would be safe, he looked down and a tear fell from his eye.

After my conversation with the doctor, I went back to speak to Syriana. As I entered, I heard her telling the nurse that I was coming in and she wanted to have some time alone to chat with me about her disease process and her hallucinations. As the nurse walked out, she asked me to sit at the foot of the bed. I was not sure why she asked so specifically, but I did as she asked, and waited for her next instruction. She told me that the nurse had told her about my openness to discuss patients' visions, and was hoping that a doctor would be open to the phenomenon. I told her I had heard many stories from my patients regarding visions as they were transitioning from this world to the next, and I explained those spiritual experiences were available to all and were meant to comfort the dying and guide them back home.

Syriana was well aware of that and wanted to make sure I would tell her story in the hope of bringing peace, hope, and love to those in difficult situations. She began to speak about a man in a long crimson robe who wore sandals and spoke about love and forgiveness. "His name was Jesus, and I first met him at the age of 12. Within weeks of meeting him, he took me into Israel and spoke of the richness of the Islamic, Jewish, and Christian faiths.

"Because I was a Muslim, I revered him as a prophet. However, in teaching me about the different faiths, he explained the fact that they all shared the same god, love, heaven, and forgiveness. Dr. Lerma, this man wore simple clothes and sandals, and I felt something in my gut he was not telling me. I did not have a bad feeling. Whatever it was he was keeping from me, made me look within for the answer. As I looked into his eyes, the feeling was so overpoweringly familiar and comforting. I had felt that feeling when I was born, and I had felt it when I was given the gifts of prophecy, love, and forgiveness."

Syriana explained that the gift of prophecy was within all. It was truly logical. For example, to know where any object is likely to move in the future, one can make an educated guess by extrapolating from the two points the object was at previously—the present and where it had been. Plotting these points and drawing a line through them and extending it outward, to almost the third or fourth point, would give you a high likelihood of occurrence. The further one extrapolated outward, the less precise the prediction. If anyone told you he had the exact date of the end of the world or even a ballpark region, he would either lying or looking too far out into the future, where everything is absolutely unwritten. Remember: Even Jesus Christ told his disciples that not even he knew the time of his return. So, when someone claims to know certain things far off in the future, he will, in all likelihood, be wrong. Most of these individuals, whether psychic, clairvoyant, telepathic, or just sane logical folk, are just seeking comfort from the woes of our world.

"For me, with respect to the bombings I was able to escape, I do not believe I escaped them as a result of clairvoyance or precognitive abilities. They were from logic. You see, when I looked back into the distant and recent past and then present, with regards to the escalating bombings of certain villages, I sensed and logically knew that there was a method to their madness, and I tapped into what their next move would entail. It is possible that I had the gift of telepathy, where I could read people's thoughts, including the terrorists close to me. The bomb that killed my family took me by surprise. I did not pick up any impending sense of doom or telepathic messages. It was likely that the scheme was planned immediately, and the culprits were not within telepathic range. I will tell you this, Dr. Lerma: Just before the bombing of my home during prayer and dinner, the prophet Jesus Christ appeared to me and my family along with a choir of angels, my grandparents, and friends, and told us we were loved very much and they were appearing to guide us back home. I saw my mother's, brother's, and sister's spirits leave their bodies, look back toward my dad and me, and they placed a bright white light around the both of us as if to protect us from something.

"The next thing I remember was a sudden bright flash of light. My father and I were being removed from the large pieces of block cement from our home. I could no longer see the light around the two of us, but we were both filled with a feeling of ecstasy. My legs were broken, and I had a punctured lung and a ruptured spleen, which had to be removed to save my life. My head was amazingly free of any injuries—not even a scratch. My father's injuries were quite severe, and similar to me, he suffered bilateral lower extremity fractures and upper extremity compound fractures. In total awe, the doctors could not believe that he, too, was without a single scratch to his head and did not sustain nerve injuries. We would both be walking within six months. God had allowed us to maintain our cerebral and cognitive functions, which today I realize was for being able to tell our story of loss, forgiveness, and love.

"During my hospital stay, the man who had visited me several times during my childhood visited me on multiple occasions. His penetrable eyes were as blue as the clear Aegean Sea on a cool summer day, with pure love exuding from them. I was hypnotized by the hope and joy that radiated from his countenance, as this willful desire somehow miraculously and completely removed all levels of discomfort. I think this was God's way of treating physical, emotional, and spiritual pain. Why use morphine when all I had to do was look into this man's eyes?"

This gentle, empathetic, and loving man explained that the removal of pain without the use of medications involved the inherent and dormant abilities of the brain to remove itself from pain of any kind. One way was to induce an out-of-body experience, allowing the spirit to separate from the body and roam free around the planet Earth, galaxies, and universes, while the painful areas of the body healed. Another way involves the ability of our brain to temporally modify, alter, and redefine the way our cerebral cortex views pain impulses. Syriana was told that human DNA, with regard to sensory mechanisms, is currently in the late phases (150 to 250 years from now) of making provisions for auto-control of all kinds of pain. That includes physical, emotional, interpersonal, and spiritual types.

Syriana felt that this prophecy had a much deeper, spiritual, and peaceful implication. The removal of this primitive and vital sensation from our brain could mean many things, but the most telling was an individual that would usher in an era of peace. The three major religious texts, the Bible, the Torah, and the Qur'an, speak of an era of total peace and love, which many theologians believe is very near and at which time the Messiah is to descend on Earth, where he will rule with total love and peace. If the alteration of our genetics is already occurring on many levels, as scientists claim, then it could be said with certain accuracy that an era of peace is on the horizon. On the contrary, it could also be said that this modification of pain perception by the brain could signal our entrance into an era of escalating pain and suffering, such as wars, financial troubles, and family and spiritual conflicts, just before our Creator is to return.

Either way, Syriana was sure that our DNA, which is dynamic, was close to unveiling its next major change in the brain's ability to respond to our higher self's requests—that is, pain reduction, telepathy, psychokinesis, lack of ego, and its ability to love without fear. This was all in response to millions of prayers and millions of years of evolution. God did not want us to have to suffer much longer in this world, so he was allowing our nervous system to evolve in such a way that humans could shut pain off or on when needed. This dynamic process, where the DNA affects its ability to add or subtract body receptors, internal body parts, and allow or disallow for the advancement and decline of paranormal cortical potential, is an area in genetics where scientists are highly engaged, and agree that many individuals are being born with this sense.

If one does not believe in our body's ability to evolve into a more efficient species, then look at the anatomical history of the appendix. Since the days of the caveman to today's evolved humans, the appendix has dramatically changed in size. In less than 40,000 years, man's appearance changed, the amount of hair on our bodies decreased, our mental capacity and cognitive functioning increased, and the average size of the appendix dropped, no longer being needed to remove hard objects (like rocks) from the intestine, which could otherwise obstruct it. Why is the body evolving? In God's infinite wisdom, he created the DNA that has the potential to hold more information than the largest computer in the world.

Many scientists and theologians believe that the answers to all of our questions lie within human DNA. Man was meant to change or evolve with his environment in order to survive. Our species was created to ask the questions: Who are we? Where do we come from? Where are we going? What are we supposed to do?

The result from our ever-changing DNA is to remove what is not needed, especially if its presence negatively affects the survival of the human species. The brain is actively learning to accomplish, with total ease, the altering of the brain's perception of pain. Syriana said that, despite the removal of her pain, she knew the electrical impulses of pain were still traveling from the injured areas of the body to the brain. However, the result was that she experienced feelings of joy. Here the brain modified the pain. Similar to any other learned cerebral process, the brain had an inherent ability to self-modify any emotion or experience.

For Syriana, because she was able to leave her body for days at a time, she was in no discomfort at all. When she left her body, she would travel with her family and angels throughout our planet, the solar system, the Milky Way Galaxy, and distant systems where life, similar to ours, exists and existed. When she asked if people on other planets believed in Jesus, she was told yes. The old man explained that certain planetary systems were much younger than hers, and as such the time period for Jesus had not arrived. Also, there were other planets where the beings were so advanced that they did not look like us and did not need to have Christ come down in human form to die for them. Instead, they had evolved to a level where there was no need for the flesh or technology, and they were helping the rest of God's civilizations. They were essentially transparent pure light energy and thought, much like the angels she had seen in the past. They communicate via telepathy, can travel to distant places via thought, and can create with their minds. Not much food is needed, as their bodies are highly efficient.

Syriana told me that human DNA held the answers to everything God wanted his children to have for a peaceful and loving life. The vast information stored in this advanced computer-type chip held in our DNA was meant to be released in phases and only to those individuals with passion for that specific data. In the late 1800s to mid-1900s, the physicist Nicolas Tesla discovered the way to bring electricity into our homes, via the alternating current. Nicolas was asked how he was able to understand current at such an early age and essentially overnight. He responded by telling his colleagues that, other than electricity being his passion, he woke up one day with the entire schematic for creating alternating and direct currents. This was definitely an example of one individual with a passion for physics and humanity whose DNA released the entire answer to his question. Einstein also talks about his dream that allowed him to discover the theory of relativity. Syriana was extremely excited about the discoveries in the near future.

During WWII, many scientists were killed in Japan and Germany, and with them died the passion for the next big discovery. Syriana went on to explain how to obtain one's personal passion. First of all, one has to be open to listening to his or her heart, which is where God-gifted desires are held. To accomplish this, the individual has to be in a relaxed mode. Because many of us are frequently anxious, stressed, insomniacs, and taking drugs that alter our brain waves, it is difficult to connect to our higher self to discover our specific passion. In this relaxed or meditative state, which I know are alpha brain waves, the brain is able to release the appropriate neuropeptide that signals the DNA to release its personal epiphany or thought formation that relates to their enthusiasm, love, and passion. The key is that one has to be in a loving and peaceful mode to trigger this chain of events. So, to obtain access to the vast information contained in our DNA, which will ultimately lead us to a happier and loving life, it is of vital importance to first self-love and self-forgive and acknowledge the one god who downloaded all potential creations into our DNA.

As Syriana and I continued speaking, I began to see her passion for humanity in the depths of her eyes. She was so excited to be talking about her experience with the angels, and the prophet she called Jesus. I asked Syriana if she believed that Jesus was the Messiah. "I still believe he is a prophet, like my Islamic faith had taught me. I believe Jesus would have told me he was the Son of God after all the time we spent together. Don't you?"

"Syriana, honestly, I will never assume to know what Jesus is thinking or wants."

Syriana looked at me in wonder and then said, "You may be right. Maybe I should not assume things as well."

Syriana and I continued our conversations about God, the political problems in Israel, and prophecies and religions for the next several days. Syriana was growing weaker and thinner, with her weight dropping to 80 pounds. Yet, she was pushing hard to continue our conversation. One of the areas she wanted to touch on had to do with 25 biblical prophecies that collectively spoke of an alignment of occurrences that would need to happen for the Messiah to appear. For the Christians and Messianic Jews, it would be the Second Coming; for the Orthodox Jews, it would be their first. This conversation reminded her of a journey she took with Jesus, while in the hospital, throughout the Middle East. From Israel to Jordan, Syria to Iraq, Syriana described her increased awareness and understanding of the peoples of the land, their plight, and their passion.

Unsure of how she was able to view things in a nonjudgmental and uncluttered way, she had a sense it was because of Jesus. For the first time, she understood the deep soul ties that Jewish,

Christian, and Islamic religions had to Jerusalem. For the Jews, this was the land promised to them by the God of Abraham and Isaac. Jerusalem was the sight of their Holy Temple, which was prophesized to be rebuilt prior to the coming of the Messiah. For the Christians, Jerusalem and other cities in Israel were where their God, Jesus Christ, was crucified, died, and buried, only to resurrect, as prophesized, in the Old and New Testaments. Christianity developed from the teachings of the Apostolic Jew, known as Paul (Saul). Indeed, there were many Jews similar to Paul who followed the teachings of Jesus Christ, but, unlike Paul, they remained Jews and not Christians. For the Muslims and Palestinian Arabs, Jerusalem was the location of the second-most holy site in the world in relation to the Prophet Muhammad. They also highly revered Jesus and Mary, but as prophets. The entire situation was too difficult for any human being to resolve, and, as such, accordance would only be achieved at the time the Messiah returned.

"Dr. Lerma, Jesus showed many things from the past and the future, which he said would help me reconcile a major issue within my heart. I am not sure what he meant, but I knew I had to keep an open and forgiving heart, if I wanted to be next to my family."

I asked her about the prophecies and her response was quick. "It is better that you research the prophecies having to do with the return of our Messiah. There are many, but you will need to write only about 25."

After asking her why I needed to locate these messages and write them down, she said that she saw that the Messiah was very near, and these 25 prophecies would bring about the evidence needed to prepare for the coming of our all-loving and all-forgiving Creator.

"It is imperative to know the signs and to carve them into your heart. There will be a sudden false sense of peace in Iraq, Israel, and even Iran, but this is the calm before the storm. Russia will be returning to inflict its dark ways on the world, by attempting to recapture and re-admit the independent provinces that broke off after the their collapse and to align with many other countries around the world. The signs will be when Russia will see a period of weakness in the United States and its allies (financial), and together with its support from certain Muslim radical organizations (Hamas, Taliban), Korea, Venezuela, Bolivia, and Iran, they will further affect the energy markets in the world. People will need to know what will occur so they can know what to pray for," Syriana firmly expressed.

Syriana was in complete control of her faculties throughout this period of time. This was completely amazing, as her organs were declining rapidly. Any individual with this degree of organ damage should have been minimally responsive, and not communicating to this degree. I had not seen her this alert, precise, and empowered, and, similar to countless other patients that experienced this type of mental surge, I knew it was God's hand and way of allowing one to give and get their final closure.

Syriana was then exhibiting signs of multi-system organ failure. For Syriana, her urine output had dropped below 5 cc's per hour, thus resulting in total body fluid overload, which would ultimately make organs such as the lungs to fill up with water, resulting in symptoms of severe shortness of breath. The arterial pulses in her feet and wrists were nonexistent, suggesting that her heart's output was negatively impacted. One would think anyone in this condition would be in distress—unless he were having a profound spiritual and pre-death experience. As a doctor I cannot explain this, and I have stopped trying to, because the result is always—and I mean always—exhilarating, peaceful, forgiving, and loving. The last sign that accompanied this physical breakdown was the vision of the spiritual realm. Syriana was looking from side to side as she smiled and laughed, with the angels on each side of her bed. "They are so beautiful, Dr. Lerma," Syriana replied quite softly and slowly.

She was increasingly tired, so I sat in the chair next to her, and told her to close her eyes and experience the love of her family, the angels, and Jesus.

I could not stop her from talking, so I just listened. Her parents and siblings were so excited to finally be uniting with her for eternity. She told me that her parents looked as if they were in their 30s, although they died at a much older age. Her siblings still looked the same age, and Jesus was older, but so handsome and loving. As she prepared to leave this world, she made sure that she had forgiven those who had killed her family, after she had forgiven herself. There was no doubt in my mind that Syriana had forgiven herself years before, because she was such a God-loving, caring, and empathetic soul.

Because her uncle was not able to spend the night with her, I made it a point to take turns with the nurses in keeping her company on her last days of life. She was sleeping almost 80 percent of the time, and did not need any sedatives for anxiety or opiates for her pain, which she continued to deny to the very end. Her last night on Earth, at about 4 a.m., she began laughing and giggling in her sleep. I was glad she was at least having comical dreams with the angels.

Before my father passed, he was laughing and smiling two to three hours before moving forward with his mom, dad, the angels, and Jesus. I quietly wondered if Syriana was two to three hours from leaving as well. She continued laughing to the point where the nurses were startled, so they entered to make sure she was okay. When they walked in and saw her smiling in her sleep, we all felt such peace. One of the three nurses who walked in noticed lots of static in the room, as the hairs on her arms and head were standing on end. In fact we all were sensing the crescendo of this type of energy.

We knew it was time, so all of us gathered around her bed, held hands, and prayed the Lord's Prayer and a Hail Mary. During the Lord's Prayer, Syriana awoke after shaking her feet. She opened her eyes and looked as though she wanted to say something, but could not. I moistened her mouth with cool water. She quickly said, "Thank you. I needed that. My lips and mouth were parched from breathing."

She was so excited and told us that Jesus had just washed her feet and told her he was ready for her. She looked at all of us with tears rolling down her face, asking us, "Don't you see him?"

"See who?" I asked Syriana.

"Jesus. He said he is Jesus Christ, who died for our sins. He was crucified and died for us, Dr. Lerma. Dr. Lerma, when he was washing my feet ever so gently and with a radiating sense of non-condemnation, I felt his wounds. When I looked up to look at his wounds, I saw all of them. They were not bleeding. They had the whitest light I have ever seen radiating from them. Before my daddy died, he told me he saw the light from his wounds as well. He is standing in front of all of us now. He is all white, and the angels, my family, and other prophets are now singing to him. Oh my! He is God! The one God! My God! I am so sorry God. I am so sorry."

All of us in the room were in awe at hearing her words and the fact that Jesus was standing next to all of us. None of us could see him, or even knew if he was present; however, we did feel love, peace, hope, faith, and forgiveness. It was palpable. With just the acknowledgment of a loving presence, we all became aware of an increasing electric charge. At that moment we all held hands, the lights suddenly turned off, and all we could see was an electrical-type charge around all of us holding hands. It turned blue to red to white. It was the most amazing thing we had ever witnessed as a group. I could also see the photons of static light transfer from our hands to each other. The interesting part was that we were not shocked in the process. We believed Syriana was telling the truth.

She looked at us and then looked to the opposite side. She tried to sit up immediately. We helped her sit up as she said, "I want to hold Jesus." She raised her arms as if in worship, said the word *Yahweh*, and fell back into her bed. Minutes later, Syriana left her body. The four of us stayed in the room for one hour, as we were no longer feeling the static. This time we smelled roses. It was Syriana's favorite. I closed my eyes and pictured her family, all the children who had passed on, Syriana, the angels, Mary, Mary Magdalene, and Jesus all running through a field with raining rose pedals!

Doctor's Notes

Syriana had permanently enriched my life with her willful desire to help me understand the power of selfless suffering, joyful forgiveness, and especially the ability to love unconditionally. By the age of 16, she encompassed these three divine attributes and exuded a level of integrity and courage I had only seen a few times in my entire life. When I pondered the people who exemplified this level of wisdom, I was humbled with the memory that most were young and terminally ill. Again, I thought about my little 9-year-old sage Matthew.

Syriana made several comments regarding the God-given gift of prophecies, but none more important than the ones relating to the coming of the Messiah. She made it clear these were not new, but many people had forgotten them, as most churches were not emphasizing their importance in the 21st century. Although not aware of the time line, she was told that an approximate time would reveal itself as the top 25 biblical prophecies would individually come to pass. The key was to know them all like the back of your hand, to carry them in one's heart, and to trust one's own God-given intuition to help decipher the message or code. Syriana was told that things that we may see, hear, and learn about the Messiah's return might not be as they seem. The ego (what some may call our sinful side) is clever and will try to separate us from the true knowledge of God's coming; yet, by relying on our inner voice of God, discernment, or gut instinct, one would remain connected to God. Syriana took extra time to discuss the true power of discernment or intuition.

"Dr. Lerma, work on your intuition daily. Find its location in your body and then listen to it and act on it. You will never be disappointed. Those with the gift of discernment or those highly sensitive to their intuition will often have the gift of prophecy as well. You see, there is a very special sensor in our body, specifically our solar plexus, which reacts to other people's emotions and intents, as well as ominous events surrounding or moving toward one. Its knowledge is primordial in nature, like our primordial needs to eat, sleep, fight or flight, and procreate. No one needs to teach us how to use these built-in life-preserving mechanisms, because they were wired in such a way that they react independently of our ability to reason.

"All of us humans have this sensor, but for whatever reason, usually ego and logic driven, most will not listen to its warning light or sounds until it's too late. For example, those pilots who choose to disregard the plane's built-in safety mechanisms, and rely on their own reasoning, have the highest rate of accidents. The bottom line is that our pride and intellect, all from the ego, are very dangerous when unopposed, especially when complacency is involved. Those without an evolved spirit fall prey to one's ego. Remember, the ego is responsible for making irrational decisions that are usually self-defeating, self-separating, compulsive, prideful, clever, and selfish."

Syriana re-emphasized the benefits of our own built-in intuitive divine device, and that it was one of the best gifts God gave us to live safe and free, so as to experience our earthly life without fear and with total joy. So, to understand the prophecies of the Bible, they are best understood with believing in God, knowledge of past and present history in the Middle East, and intuition or discernment. In the end, trust your gut instinct.

Part II

Further Research

Conclusion

Within every fiber of my being, I am comforted by faith in knowing that our Creator will work for eternity if need be, to bring every soul he created back to the home we will all share as brothers and sisters for eternity. It was this final and joyful truth of unification that resonated the loudest and the clearest within my scientific mind and empathetic heart. Whether my patients were from different races and cultures, perceived or identified themselves as being pious or non-pious, life-givers or life-takers, atheists or agnostics, new-age thinkers or old-age thinkers, believers or non-believers, homosexuals or heterosexuals, lovers or fighters, the one constant observation that I discovered was the similarities in their visual, emotional, and spiritual experiences as they were about to leave this world. Their final visions and messages all came from a loving, spiritual world, which has existed around us and in us since the beginning of time. The message of love, forgiveness, non-condemnation, and non-judgment mentioned day in and day out is constant, no matter what one does or thinks. What is not constant is our own psyche. It is this psyche, or ego versus our higher spirit, where the real battle exists. Most of my patients went on to reveal that humans would never find eternal peace through their own selfish actions. True lasting peace can only manifest itself around us and within us when one's spiritual essence connects to the Source and yearns to experience heaven on Earth.

So, do not be hard on yourselves. Remember: We all have a selfish ego, which does its own selfish things, and for reasons unclear to us. It's a daily process of acknowledging both its existence and purpose in altering our soul. Love the ego for its value in helping transform our essence into that of an enduring and loving soul, which in the end will be free to lovingly unify with the Creator of all.

Latest Medical Research on Pre-Death Visions

Despite the submission of thousands of near-death and pre-death case studies from physicians in North America and Europe, which report non-hallucinatory-type visions from both terminally ill patients during their final phase of the dying process (PDE), and from those who have been revived after a cardiac arrest (NDE), the majority of the medical community is still opposed to the consideration that the energy of our consciousness, which some refer to as the intangible part of our brain, could conceivably continue to exist after the death of the tangible form. Still, there are several physicians and physicists who continue to advance steadily in obtaining answers to the four questions man has asked for thousands of years: Who are we? Where do we come from? Where are we going? And, what are we supposed to do? This chapter will review the latest NDE and

PDE research being carried out by physicians around the world, as well as me, and future studies, which will involve major universities.

Description of Near-Death and Pre-Death Experiences

Most would comment about floating above everyone in the emergency room or area they had died in, and usually close to the right or left corner of the room up toward the ceiling. The experience usually left them with a deep sense of peace, love, and security. Many of my patients who reported an out-of-body experience in the emergency room, often described their awareness of being dead and hearing and seeing the medical personnel who were working on their body. Their description of the people inside and outside of the trauma room, including what they said they were wearing and their names from their work badges, were almost always eerily correct. For many, this was proof that consciousness continues after ones heart stops. For many others, this only proved that the moment of death is not solely dependent on cardiac arrest. Either way, both groups agreed on the fact that there was need to study the brain at the moment of death.

The following is a case study of a patient of mine who I spoke of in my first book, *Into The Light.* I had a patient who arrived into the emergency room with chest pain. Mr. M was in is 70s, an alcoholic with a long history of being physically abusive to his family. Shortly after he was placed in the trauma room, he lost consciousness as a result of a lethal cardiac arrhythmia. The EKG revealed an anterolateral myocardial infarct—a massive heart attack. He coded several times while in the emergency room, and each time, I shocked him back to life. He was stabilized and eventually recuperated.

Shortly after his heart attack, Mr. M told me about his out-of-body experience and said he could likely prove it, as he remembered seeing a 1985 quarter on the top of the 9-foot-tall rhythm monitor while he floated above his body. Mr. M wanted me to confirm his experience. Out of curiosity, I obliged and climbed up a ladder to look for the quarter on the monitor that had displayed his heart rhythm just a few days before. Sure enough, the 1985 quarter was lying amongst the light film of dust and in the lower-right-hand corner, as he said it would be. The year was right as was its location. Mr. M was so excited when I confirmed what he had seen. As I sat and talked to him, he went on to tell a phenomenal story. He spoke of a loving voice coming from the bright light along the right corner of the room, which if he wanted, would be allowed to return to mend his personal problems with himself first, and then his family. Desiring to find forgiveness for his past actions, Mr. M chose to return. He described his out-of-body experience as surreal, and wanted it to be true with the hopes of recalling most of the beautiful and loving conversations he had with the light being. Aware of his demise, he wanted to make sure this was not a hallucination or illusion, so he looked around the trauma room for something only he could see and would be able to get confirmation from one of the medical staff after he returned. His life would not be the same, as well as the lives of everyone present that day.

Many were told they would come back, as it was not their time. They were often told they had much more of life to experience so their afterlife would be more fruitful and full of joy and love. Most did not want to come back, but a gentle nudge by large blue to white loving beings, as well as a visual reminder of the unfinished business on Earth they had agreed to long ago, almost always changed their will. The spirit light told them that God's plan was beyond their wildest imagination. Many recall being told by their deceased loved ones that we are never alone and not to fear God, as he is that unawakened part of us that does not know hatred, jealousy, anger, selfishness, revenge, egoism, condemnation, or judgment. They emphasized that all these attitudes and personality traits come from our sinful self, the ego. It is the self-defeating and self-separating ego that humans need to recognize within others and ourselves and defeat through understanding, in order to awaken the God within.

The terminally ill have some of the same experiences, but while still alive. These experiences begin around four weeks before one's transition, and continue to the last breath. The spiritual beings many of the patients see, come to help one cross to the next spiritual realm by helping with forgiveness and love of oneself first, then others. This closure allows the soul to leave its physical body with ease.

The terminally ill do not immediately see the tunnel of light until the last one to three days of life. In pre-death experiences, the spiritual beings come to the patients' environment. In near-death experiences, the deceased travel toward the spiritual beings that are in the bright tunnel of white light.

Secular belief by the vast majority of the medical profession

The two types of experiences previously mentioned continue to be categorized by a large portion of the medical profession as mere hallucinations of the dying brain. Many physicians and physiologists, and genetic engineers, believe these false perceptions are thought to be conjured by the complex cerebral cortex, with the genetic driven purpose of comforting one's higher consciousness and even the divisive, self-absorbed ego, as they both unwillingly prepare to usher in its destiny—a destiny created by scientists who would rather believe in an abyss filled with no family, no friends, no joy, no love, and especially no existence. Ironically, these same people on their deathbed end up refuting their previous claims only to be replaced with assertions to the contrary. With everything I have seen, felt, and objectively documented, there is absolutely no way that our spiritual essence goes into oblivion when we die. As a scientist myself, I am fully aware of a scientist's oath to only provide data that is ultimately accepted as fact by a unanimous consensus of one's extremely critical colleagues, yet I understand now that, no matter how close any scientist, including me, gets to proving the existence of God, science alone will not be enough. To bridge this gap will ultimately necessitate something intangible and incalculable: faith.

Unlocking Untapped Brain Powers

Since my last book was released the American Board of Medical Specialties, under pressure by primary care physicians, hospitals, insurance companies, and the general public, agreed that a new specialty of medicine (Hospice and Palliative Medicine) was urgently needed to address the needs of the "Whole Person," with emphasis on the terminally ill. The major concern was that most physicians were not adequately trained and indifferent with regard to treating the four types of pain frequently experienced by the terminally ill (physical, emotional, interpersonal, and spiritual pain). With this medical specialty in place, the funding for research is now in place and medical institutions in Virginia, Arizona, Texas, Canada, England, and Germany have begun to explore the brain as it relates to near death experiences (NDEs), pre-death experiences (PDEs), hallucinations as opposed to visions of the terminally-ill, extrasensory perception looking at telepathy, clairvoyance, and precognition, and the role of dimethyltryptamine (DMT) as it relates to visions of the dying and alien abduction experience. Dr. Peter Fenwick, a highly regarded neuropsychiatrist in England, was able to reproduce the results from an American study, which concluded there is some evidence that suggests that telepathy, although weak, does in fact exist.

Before Einstein died, he commented that one day man would unlock the secrets and unlimited power of the brain, no longer needing phones, cars, or planes. That man would attain the ability to telepathically communicate with others and teleport oneself by mere thought and will to any place in the cosmos. Einstein believed the brain was no more than an extremely complex and spiritual computer, with capabilities of sending information via electromagnetic and gravitational energies to another human brain. If today's computers, which are an extension of man, can connect without the use of wires, then why can't the human brain, which created them, do the same? I am sure continued research in this field will prove Einstein correct once more.

Research Differentiating Hallucinations From the Visions of the Dying

The research data I am getting ready to publish defines the differences between hallucinations and pre-death experiences (PDEs). Hallucinations, which denote an abnormal sensory activity in the area of the cortex, are not based on physical perception and not shared between people. The most frequent causes are drugs (opiates and sedatives), liver failure, kidney failure, fevers, urinary and bowel impaction, and brain tumors. Treatment of these disease states will usually eliminate periods of disorientation and combativeness. During the episodes of NLCA or pre-death visions, the patients most often have a clear consciousness based on physical perception and are shared between people in the same physical condition. These visions differ vastly from hallucinations on several levels, as seen on the following chart.

	Pre-Death Visions	Hallucinations
Visions herald death	Yes	No
Delirium	Yes	No
Treatable causes	Yes	No
Initial visions greater than four seconds	Yes	No
Comforting in nature	Yes	No
Recalling ability	Yes	No
Spiritual in nature	Yes	No
Confusing speech	Yes	No
Physically combativeness	Yes	No
Visions of deceased only	Yes	No
Visions of the living	Yes	No
Prophetic messages	Yes	No
Resolved by treatment of infection	Yes	No
Joyous demeanor	Yes	No
Anxious/psychotic	Yes	No

Earthly visions alone	Yes	No
Heavenly and angelic visions	Yes	No
Conscious of two realities	Yes	No
Leads to conflict resolution	Yes	No
Often acquire telepathy	Yes	No
Often acquire clairvoyance	Yes	No
Often acquire precognition	Yes	No
Feel enlightened	Yes	No
Lasts 24 hours a day, for five days, pre-death	Yes	No
Survival value	Yes	No
Independent of Pathology/drugs	Yes	No
*Shared Visions	Less often	Never

*Shared visions have been documented where one or more families or friends present at the bedside of a patient having a pre-death experience, will report seeing exactly the same images. This occurs less than10 percent of the time.

State-of-the-Art Neural Imaging in Evaluating ESP and Pre-Death Experiences or Visions

The Central Intelligence Agencies science division conducted ESP experiments in the mid- to late 20th century, and proved that certain humans were likely born with this aptitude and were often capable of reading people's thoughts and the future, and, less often, claimed to be in communication with beings of an alternate dimension or world within reach of ours. Clearly, this research was fascinating. Today, technology being used to pinpoint which part of the brain may be responsible for these abilities includes neuro-imaging scans of the MEG (Magnetoelectoencephalography) scan and f-MRI (functional-Magnetic Resonance Imaging) scan, cutting-edge tools in understanding which locale of cerebral neurons (if any) work together to create a multitude of occurrences, including seizures, hallucinations, visions of spirits, and deceased loved ones.

In a study I preformed recently, using imaging to attempt to determine which parts of the brain were active during hallucinations related to morphine (pain killer) and lorazepam (sedative), along with spiritual visions, the preliminary studies were similar to the predicted results. I predicted that, in a hallucinatory state, as in drug-related delirium, that the neurons from varying parts of the brain would be releasing magnetic energy signals at varying times, essentially, in a piece meal type pattern. The predicted results for the five patients having visions of spirits and deceased loved ones would likely involve the temporal lobes and right hemisphere.

The temporal lobes have been shown to house ESP abilities and spiritual experiences. The right hemisphere is where creativity and imagination reside. The left hemisphere is more analytical and logical, so less likely to be working during a pre-death experience. The largest obstacle I encountered with regard to this study was getting the delirious patients to comply, and getting the pre-death experience group down to the radiology department before the visions lapsed. Unfortunately, of the 30 potential patients including controls that had agreed to partake in the study, only five were stable enough to endure the test. Despite this setback, I was astounded with the tentative results, which revealed a significant positive predictive value. In other words, the predictions made were very close to what was actually reported. Of the five patients, three were having visions of their deceased relatives and spiritual guides; the other two were delirious, one of whom was having hallucinations of spiders and scorpions, while the other was in a Volkswagen beetle with Jerry Springer and Judge Judy. The two hallucinatory patients scans revealed a schizophrenic-type pattern throughout the brain. The results of the three patients having pre-death experiences were quite fascinating.

Patient #1, who was dying of prostate cancer, was having visions of Mother Mary and his deceased mother and father. After the exam, he told the medical staff and myself that "God will one day soon reveal the powers of the brain he created to all of you. He is so joyful that all of you care enough to understand his creations as well as comforting the sick. He loves all of you with every ounce of energy that he has created in this universe and will continue to create. He is smiling and hugging all of you and wants all of you to smile, hug, and love others the same way." Some dismissed his comments as nonsense, but most believed what he told them was true. I wanted to believe.

One X-ray technician said, "To think that we just received a message from God and he held us in his arms, that's unfathomable. I know I felt it. I can even smell roses. Doesn't anyone else? I will never forget this day." Two other technicians smelled the roses and all of us felt a minor amount of static electricity around the X-ray room. There was no doubting the changed electrical energy in the room. We quickly repeated his scan and noticed something I had never seen before. The first scan showed both temporal lobes quite active. The second was beyond remarkable, in that more than 60 percent of the brain showed simultaneous activity. Is it possible that the ability to visualize our Creator with our eyes calls for the simultaneous firing of most of our neurons, as was seen with this patient? If Einstein simultaneously used 10 percent of his brain to come up with the theory of relativity, then what could 20 percent do? How about 100 percent? Had God just told us that we were on the right path toward creating heaven on Earth? What was it that allowed those within days to less than four weeks of dying to see their deceased loved ones, the angels, and God? Matthew, a young patient of mine with retinal cancer, told me, "If God knows you are searching for the truth with loving intentions, which in reality is God, you will be led down the rainbow to his pot of gold."

I knew it was the balance between the two of everything in this world that aided one in experiencing heaven on Earth. The two hemispheres of the brain are mirror images of itself, which are connected by the corpus callosum.

The study of patient #1 revealed that a significant percentage of both hemispheres were working together, so it was likely that they needed to function together in order to have PDEs or NDEs. The angels that patient #1 saw told him that the human brain is rapidly evolving to reveal new powers. In fact, thousands of children being born today already have the capacity to experience both realities. That was interesting, as two of my friends recently told me that their 4-year-old nephew and 6-year-old granddaughter were talking about seeing people in another world next to ours and were being given messages for humanity. They asked me to meet them and see what I thought. To this day I have not had a chance to speak with them, but I will now make it a point to get it done. A wonderful book entitled *Children of Now* explains this phenomenon in great detail.

Patient #2, who was blind since birth and who was dying of ovarian cancer, was equally as remarkable as patient #1. She claimed to be seeing colors and people for the first time in her life. Her scans revealed a highly active occipital lobe, the area responsible for vision. The temporal lobes were noted to be equally as active. There have been a few cases documented where terminally ill blind patients were able to decipher colors and objects as a result of spiritual visions. Several were even able to draw what they were seeing. Truly amazing!

Patient #3 was a 16-year-old boy with osteosarcoma or bone cancer, who had been having visions of the afterlife for more than two weeks. He knew his time was almost up in this world, and, as such, wanted to be part of the study. He said he wanted to help science and the world learn more about the love and joy on the "other side" he was privileged to experience while in his body. I attained 80 percent of the predicted results. His scans again showed the temporal lobes lighting up.

Like anything in our body, for any system to function properly, it takes a whole host of delicately refined mechanisms. Theoretically, for the pre-death experience or extrasensory perception to operate, it would likely include the incorporation of certain neurons and then a specific amount of neuropeptides and neurohormones, such as serotonin levels (5HT), dimethyltryptamine (DMT), dopamine, and endorphin levels.

EEG Monitors and the PDE/ NDE Signature Brain Pattern

A recent scientific study in the United States (University of Virginia) and England by a neuropsychiatrist named Peter Fenwick MD, using EEG monitors attached to two people in separate rooms, one of which was exposed to a strobe light, revealed an evoked potential as follows:

A.) Patient #1 was placed in an isolated room, had an EEG wrapped around her cranium room, and was exposed to a strobe light that fired at a specific rate and time. The EEG monitor had the expected result of an evoked potential, or a spike when the strobe light was activated.

B.) Patient #1 was then asked to merely think about patient #2. Patient #2 was also asked to think about patient #1 and what the experiment entailed. After 30 minutes, Patient #2's EEG monitor resulted in an evoked potential of nearly the same amplitude (height) and duration as patient #1.

C.) The findings were astounding and provided evidence that quantum physics, including quantum entanglement, as well as the unified field theory, offered support to explain that we are all indeed connected down to the subatomic level. This could also add credence to the biblical statement "Where two or more are gathered in my name, I AM in the midst." The actual definition of quantum entanglement is as follows: Quantum entanglement is a phenomenon in which the states of two or more physical bodies are linked together so that one object can no longer be adequately described without full mention of its counterpart— it's as though both physical bodies are so intertwined by a force, that, even though they are spatially separated, the force connecting them makes them one. It's uncanny how Jesus' parable and the Law of Quantum Entanglement are basically saying the same thing. The difference is that quantum entanglement proves what can happen if two objects (humans) connect because of familiarity (similar belief), if there appears a force (GOD) that makes them all one while allowing both to retain their individuality (free will).

Another example of quantum physics explaining Jesus' message is when the apostles ask Jesus where heaven was. Most thought it was large and expansive, yet Jesus told them it was essentially was the size of a mustard seed (one of the smallest seeds around the Holy Land), which when planted grows to be very large. Well, how can heaven be in a small seed? I am sure God was explaining its unlimited potential energy that could create anything. The seed, in reality, is likely referring to the general law of quantum physics, which states that nature's most potent forces and energy are carried via the smallest unit of quanta (the seed). Fascinating how Jesus was describing quantum mechanics 2,000 years before man new it existed. This makes me wonder how many more undiscovered mathematical and physics laws are mentioned throughout the Bible. In my first book, there are several stories where my patients mentioned "there were more messages and knowledge Jesus wanted us to have to improve our lives. However, in order for these messages to be revealed, one had to invoke the parable of entanglement." Man needed to come to terms with his ego (unconsciousness/self-serving), and his spirit (consciousness/empathy), so that God and his knowledge would manifest within. The Christian Bible, the Qur'an, the Torah, the Buddhist texts, and other great books all speak the language of quantum physics.

D.) This experiment could explain why when one person thinks of another, a call or e-mail from him or her arrives shortly thereafter. My mother and I frequently experience this phenomenon. When an unexpected thought of my mother enters my mind, I usually end up calling her, only to find out she was thinking about me and wanted to talk to me. This has happened so often that she expects a call every time she thinks of me. If I don't, I end up picking up other messages. I love my mother deeply, and cherish this gift God has given us. In sum, thoughts from one person are likely transferred to a specific person or specific group of people, often having the desired effect as requested by the sender of the thought or request. The desired effect is dependent on the person receiving the information and whether he chooses to act on it. My patients tell me that this is one way in which departed souls communicate with us, and possibly how we communicate with God and how he communicates with us.

B Facts About the Ego and Higher Awareness

Ego: An exaggerated sense of one's own importance and a feeling of superiority to other people.

Higher-awareness: Part of our non-ego-based identity, which is empowered by the values that connect us to God.

	Ego	Higher Awareness
1. Attains purpose and employment via:	Negativity	Inner Joy
	Find faults	Find good
	Hurting	Helping
	Manipulation	
2. Believes in self-sacrifice in order to help others:	Yes	No
3. Has a false sense of Self:	Yes	No

		Ego	Higher Awareness
4.	Is self-defeating and self-separating:	Yes	No
5.	Can reason through intelligence:	Yes	No
6.	Was doomed from the beginning of its inception, as it survives from identification with its enemies and its own selfish goals:	Yes	No
7.	Created religion to define itself and to foster separation of man from man, and man from God:	Yes	No
8.	Is unifying and accepts that man was made in God's image:	Yes	No
9.	Defines itself through its: enemies	Self	God
10.	Carries attributes of anger, hatred, jealousy, entitlement, and bitterness:	Yes	No
11.	Strengthened by anger, joy, manipulation, helping others, resentment, and compassion.	Yes	No
12.	Religious leaders consider it evil, sinful, dark, and clever:	Yes	No
13.	Is compulsive and clever:	Yes	No
14.	Is patient and transparent:	Yes	No

	Ego	Higher Awareness
15. Most politicians and some religious leaders:	Yes	No

16. One's identity should shift from the ego (the physical mind) to our higher awareness (our divine spirit) early in one's life. The awakening of our higher awareness allows one to connect to God. The ego is destined to shrink and dissolve through time leaving one's divine spirit to finally become one with love, peace, forgiveness, and joy. In other words, while one's spirit resides in the physical body, hope is placed in our higher awareness to reconcile the ego and the spirit in such a way, which makes God real within. It is this achievement and realization that allows for a joyful and fruitful life and transition from earth to heaven.

17. Is created by the mind:	Yes	No
18. Continually is struggling for survival. Ironically, it is self-destructive:	Yes	No
18. Created a mental God one had to believe in:	Yes	No
19. Finds God through personal enlightenment and not via an mental image:	Yes	No

20. Dividing versus unifying: The ego divides through its love for violence, hatred, jealousy, entitlement, and self-righteousness.

Examples are religious wars and the political arena. Our spiritual or higher self is purely unifying, forgiving, and non-condemning. Our higher awareness wants to end violence and hatred through the realization that all humans are connected and one with God. The importance of reconciling the ego and divine spirit through our higher awareness or enlightenment was revealed by Jesus to Mary Magdalene after his resurrection. Around AD 320, the Council of Nicea, which was established to generate a Bible for Roman Christians, was accused of bigotry and intentionally keeping many Christian books from being added to the Bible. One of those books was the Gospel of Mary Magdalene. It was this gospel that spoke about Jesus' resurrection and his first conversation with Mary Magadalene. It was written by others close to her that she spoke about meeting with Jesus and being told to teach others the importance of finding his love and forgiveness by reconciling our dark and immature side (ego) with our divine side (higher awareness). Using free will to accept this reunification and healing of the two would automatically awaken the kingdom of God within our body.

It is believed by several scholars that the early church leaders struck the Gospel of Mary Magdalene from the Bible for fear of losing control of the masses. These self-appointed leaders of God's word wanted everyone to believe that the road to heaven was attained through strict obedience. Self-enlightenment or awakening of the God within, as described by Mary Magdalene, was viewed as sinful.

21. As the ego strengthens itself, it replaces the awakened self with other ideologies and belief systems that only serve to enhance a false-sense of self. The ego continually fights to define our identity through right and wrong. The reality is that the ego is always wrong and ultimately self-destructive and collectively destructive.

22. The greatest achievement of man is not science, technology, or music, but the recognition of its own self-destructive behavior and the desire to transcend it.

23. Being awakened or enlightened to God's promises and love enhances a true sense of joy.

24. Many of my patients spoke about having to view glimpses of the absolute truth within themselves during their life review. Reconciling their ego with their higher-self made this difficult for many to accept. I do remember several patients not achieving this level of growth before their death. It was very difficult to watch. Theses same patients were told that the mere attempt to rise above the ego was enough to insure a joyful transition back home. Yet, because of today's egocentric society, many opt to continue living ego-centered lives.

25. Another message from the angels: "To see God, one must use his free will to become intimate with one's inner goodness, which is essentially God."

26. Uses the mind through thoughts
    to carry out its agenda: Yes   No

27. Pope John Paul II believed in the transcendence from the egocentric thought of today's religions to our higher self by realizing that there are many paths toward God. As Pope John Paul II said, "After all, Jesus visited prostitutes, Jewish leaders, tax collectors, politicians, non-believers, murderers, and many otherEastern religious leaders."

Finding Self-Forgiveness and Self-Love

The way to God is through self-forgiveness. The way to self-forgiveness is through self-love. The way to self-love is through seeking God.

—Dr. John Lerma

I. To be self-forgiving is to:

- Entertain the thought of an all-loving and all-forgiving God.

- Let go of your self-anger for past mistakes and failures.

- No longer need to punish yourself or have regret(s) over agonizing issues created by your reluctant action(s).

- Love oneself, which is the same as loving the kingdom of God within.

- Accept oneself as a perfect being created despite your past failures and mistakes.

- Attempt spiritual self-healing of one's heart by calming self-rejection, quieting the sense of failure, and lightening the burden of guilt.

- STOP the need of having to work so hard to make up for one's past offenses.

II. Without self-forgiveness, one runs the risk of:

- Unresolved hurt, pain, and suffering from self-destructive behaviors.

- Unresolved guilt and remorse for self-inflicted offenses.

- Chronically seeking revenge and paybacks toward yourself.

- Being caught up in unresolved self-anger, self-hatred, and self blaming.

- Pessimism and negativity becoming one's identity.

- Having a festering wound that never allows the revitalization of self-healing.

- Fear over making new mistakes or of having the old mistakes revealed.

- Being overwhelmed by fear of failure, fear of rejection, fear of non-approval, low self-esteem, and low self-worth.

III. Lack of self-forgiveness can result in:

- A loss of love for yourself.

- Indifference toward yourself and your needs.

- An emotional vacuum in which little or no emotions are shown or shared.

- Chronic attacks or angry outbursts against the self.

- Disrespectful treatment of self.

- Self-destructive behaviors.

- Self-pitying.

- Suspicions about others' motives, behaviors, attitudes, and beliefs when they are accepting of you.

- Depression and anxiety.

- Chronic hostility and cynicism.

- Self-demeaning behaviors.

- Unwillingness to change and/or unwillingness to seek the help necessary to change.

IV. Statements made by those who feel they do not deserve to be forgiven:

- Self-conviction: God should never forgive me for what I have done. I should suffer.

- If something bad happens to me, I know it is God punishing me for my sins.

- I am sick over what I did; how can I ever forgive myself, let alone God?

- I must be inherently evil, and I am despicable. No forgiveness will ever change that.

- It is a sign of weakness or softness to forgive myself.

- I must always keep my guard up so as never to repeat my wrongdoings.

- I am just seeking my forgiveness so that I can come back and hurt myself again.

- I do not deserve any self-kindness, self-compassion, or self-forgiveness for what I have done to myself or others.

- I resent myself for hurting myself and others.

- If I could treat myself or others that way, then I am undeserving of being forgiven, loved, or cared for.

V. In order to forgive yourself one needs to practice:

- Believing and trusting in our loving God to take over the burden and to lead you during this and other hurtful periods.

- Praying and meditating not only to accept my weaknesses, but to also accept my strengths, my goodness, and my inherent ability to love and forgive, and to accept the all-loving and all-forgiving God within.

- Allowing yourself to be loved by the ones who love you unconditionally: your family and God.

- Letting go of past hurt and pain.

- Trusting in your goodness.

- Letting go of fears for the future.

- Taking a risk to change and have fun. Awareness of the constant errors we will commit as a human being, with an intent to understand why and how to avert them in the future is vital.

- Letting go of self-destructive behaviors, such as drug and alcohol abuse, anorexia, bulimia, overlooking slight relapses, or steps backward. Remember that God forgives an infinite number of times because he loves us dearly and knows we were born to make mistakes for our growth. Just become aware of that greater power within that will truly love you and forgive you, even beyond that which you are capable of doing, and he will do the rest. We have to continue the process of self-forgiveness with the understanding that we will always be fallible, as long as we are in this human body.

- Developing trust in yourself.

- Open, honest, and assertive communication with yourself concerning hurts, pains, and offenses experienced.

- Identifying and replacing the irrational beliefs that block your ability to forgive yourself.

VI. Steps to develop self-forgiveness.

Step 1: In order to increase your ability to forgive yourself, you need to recognize what this behavior involves. Answer the following questions:

- What do you mean by "self forgiveness"?

- Have you ever forgiven yourself before? How did it feel?

- Have you ever brought up something from the past to remind you how you hurt yourself or others? How did that make you feel?

- How has the absence of forgiving yourself affected your current emotional stability and your relationship with yourself, others, and God?

- What are the signs of the absence of self forgiveness in your relationship with your: (1) family of origin, (2) current family, (3) significant others, (4) spouse, (5) children, (6) parents, (7) relatives, (8) friends, and (9) coworkers?

- With whom do you experience a wall or barrier behind which you hide your past real or perceived failures, mistakes, errors, or misdeeds? What feedback do you get about this wall you have been hiding behind?

- What beliefs block your ability to forgive yourself? What would be necessary to change these beliefs?

- What new behaviors do you need to develop in order to increase your ability to forgive yourself?

- What role does the existence of spirituality play in your ability to forgive yourself? The lack of it?

- For what do you need to forgive yourself?

Step 2: Now that you have a better picture of what is involved in self-forgiveness, you are ready to work on a specific past failure, mistake, or misdeed. List a failure, mistake, error, misdeed, or event for which you are unable to forgive yourself. Answer the following questions:

- How much energy, creativity, problem-solving capability, and focus on growth is sapped from you whenever you recall this past hurt?

- What feelings come to mind as you recall this past hurt?

- How would you describe your role in this past event? In what ways were you the victim, perpetrator, enabler, martyr, bystander, instigator, target, scapegoat, distracter, peacemaker, people-pleaser, or rescuer?

- Why do you feel strongly over what happened and how you treated yourself or others?

- What did this event do to your self-esteem and self-worth?

- Who was responsible for your reaction to the incident?

- Who was responsible for your feelings about the incident?

- Who was responsible for your inability to forgive yourself?

- How can you forgive yourself?

- How can you put this incident behind you?

- How can you avoid being so hurt when something like this happens again?

Step 3: Once you have thought out how to forgive yourself for this past mistake, failure, error, or event, use this self-forgiveness mirror work script. For the next 30 days let go of your self-anger, self-blaming, self-hatred, self-disgust, and self-pity over this specific past event by spending time in front of a mirror using this script.

VII. Self-Forgiveness Dialogue With Oneself. Closing one's eyes in a quiet place helps tremendously. At first, it will be difficult, and one may not get through the entire exercise. However, repeated hopeful attempts will bring remove the victim mentality and replace it with the victor or victorious essence deep within.

- I forgive you for (the past event). Our all-loving God has forgiven me for everything I have done and will ever do.
- You are a human being subject to making mistakes and errors.
- You do not need to be perfect in order for me to love you.
- This (past event) is just an example of the challenges which you have. You will meet the challenge and grow by handing the pain and hurt from this problem (past event) over to God.
- You are a good person. I love you.
- You deserve my understanding, compassion, and forgiveness.
- You deserve to come out from behind the wall you have built around yourself as a result of this (past event).
- I love seeing you, talking to you, and listening to you.
- You have within you all you need to grow in self-esteem. There is nothing you have ever done that can't be forgiven by God and me.
- You did the best you could, knowing what you did at the time.
- You have compulsive and impulsive habitual ways of acting, which you are working to change.

- You may have slip ups again and again, but, as long as you get back on the wagon of recovery and keep on trying, that's good enough for me.

- You no longer need to condemn yourself for this (past event).

- You are forgiven. I love you and I am so happy to have you in my life.

- You and I are best friends and together we will gain strength by giving all our past hurt, pain, guilt, self-anger, and self-hatred over to God our Father.

- I feel lighter as we talk because I feel the burden of the hurt, pain, and guilt over this (past event) lifting from my shoulders.

- I see you holding your head up and standing taller as I forgive you for this (past event).

- I know that Jesus Christ has forgiven you, and I feel the peace and serenity of letting go of the need to hold on to it (past event) anymore.

- I forgive you because you deserve to be forgiven. No one needs to hold onto such a burden for so long.

- You deserve a better life, instead of the bitter one, than have been giving yourself.

- Let go of this (past event) and know that you are forgiven.

- You are a loveable, capable, special person, and I promise to continue to work on letting go of hurt and pain from the past which has been preventing your inner-healing and self-growth.

Step 4: Once you have forgiven yourself fully over the past occurrences, repeat Step 3, addressing one at a time all the past or present actions of hurting self or others for which you need to forgive yourself.

Step 5: When you have exhausted and repeatedly voiced your list of incidents or victim issues for which you need self-forgiveness, you will be on the road to developing a disposition of the new you, the victor(ious)-self.

Bibliography

Aczel, Amir D. *Probability: Why There Must Be Intelligent Life in the Universe.* New York: Harcourt Brace, 1998.

Adolphs, R.D. Tranel, and A.R. Damasio. "The Human Amydala in Social Judgment." *Nature* (1998): 470–74

Altman, Stuart A. "The Structure of Primate Social Communication." In *Social Communication Among Primates.* Chicago: University of Chicago Press, 1967.

Ameisen, Jean Claude. "The Origin of Programmed Cell Death." *Science* (1996): 1278–9.

Ashmarin, I.P. "Neurological Memory as a Probable Product of Evolution of Other Forms of Biological Memory." *Zhurnal Evoiutsionnoi Biokhimii I Fiziolgii* (1973): 217–24.

Axelrod, Robert. *The Complexity of Cooperation: Agent-Based Models of Competition and Collaboration.* Princeton, N.J.: Princeton University Press, 1997.

Bailey, Alice. *Telepathy and the Etheric Vehicle.* New York: Lucis Press, 1950.

Barianaga, Marcia. "Watching the Brain Remake Itself." *Science* (1994): 1475.

Begley, Sharon. "Science Finds God." *Newsweek*, July 20, 1998.

Carlson, Richard F. *Science and Christianity: Four Views*. Downers Grove, Ill.: InterVarsity Press, 2000.

Cohen, John. "Novel Center Seeks to Add Spark to Origin of Life." *Science* 270 (1995): 1925–26.

Craig, William Lane and Quentin Smith. *Theism, Atheism, and Big Bang Cosmology*. Oxford: Clarendon Press, 1993.

Damasio, Antonio R. "How the Brain Creates the Mind." *Scientific American*, December 1999.

Davies, Paul. *Superforce: The Search for a Grand Unified Theory of Nature*. New York: Simon and Schuster, 1984.

Fenwick, Dr. Peter, and Elizabeth Fenwick. *The Art of Dying*. London: Continuum, 2008.

Funk, Robert W., and Roy W. Hoover. *The Jesus Seminar, the Five Gospels*. San Francisco: Harper San Francisco, 1993.

Hawking, Stephen. *A Brief History of Time*. New York: Bantam Books, 1998.

Hick, John. *Death and Eternal Life*. London: William Collins & Sons, 1976.

Kaku, Michio. *Introduction to Superstrings and M-Theory*. New York: Springer-Verlag, 1999.

Kuebler Ross, E. *On Death and Dying*. New York: Macmillan, 1969.

Lemly, Brad. "Why is There Life?" *Discover*, November 2002.

Lindsted, Dr. Robert. *The Power of the Cross*. Wichita, Kansas: Bible Truth, Inc., 2000.

Moreland, J.P. *Christianity and the Nature of Science*. Grand Rapids, Mich.: Baker, 1989.

Popper, Karl R., and John C. Eccles. *The Self and its Brain*. New York: Springer-Verlag, 1977.

Provine, William. "Scientists Face It! Science and Religion are Incompatible." *The Scientist* 2 (1998).

Russell, Bertrand. *Why I am Not a Christian?* New York: Simon & Schuster, 1957.

Simpson, George Gaylord. *The Meaning Of Evolution*. Cambridge, Mass.: Harvard University Press, 1967.

Strobel, Lee. *The Case for Faith*. Grand Rapids, Mich,: Zondervan Press, 2000.

————. *A Journalist Investigates Scientific Evidence That Points Toward God*. Grand Rapids, Mich.: Zondervan Press, 2005.

Templeton, John. *The Humble Approach: Scientists Discover God*. Philadelphia, Penn.: Templeton Foundation, 1998.

Wertheim, Margaret. "The Pope's Astrophysicist." *Wired*, December 2002.

Wilder, Penfield. *The Mystery of the Mind*. Princeton, N.J.: Princeton University Press, 1975.

Woodward, Kenneth L. "Faith Is More Than A Feeling." *Newsweek*, May 7, 2001.

Index

About the Author

John Lerma, MD, currently serves as a consultant for several hospices and palliative units in Houston and San Antonio, Texas. He is widely known for his compassionate and loving care of hundreds of terminally ill patients, as well as his tenure as the inpatient medical director for the internationally renowned Medical Center Hospice of Houston, Texas. Because the inpatient unit is located in the heart of the largest medical center in the world, he has worked closely with MD Anderson Hospital, the leading cancer institute in the world in research and teaching.

After obtaining a degree in pharmacy at the University of Texas at Austin, he entered medical school at the University of Texas San Antonio and, years later, finished his training in internal medicine. Over the last 10 years he has focused his career in the field of hospice and palliative medicine.

Board-certified in internal medicine as well as hospice and palliative medicine, Dr. Lerma is recognized for his compassionate care of hospice and palliative patients as well as research in the field of pre-death experiences. While working at the Medical

Center in Houston, he was involved with teaching hospice and palliative medicine to medical students, residents, and geriatric, oncology, and palliative fellows from several institutions. As an international speaker, Dr. Lerma is recognized for his signature lecture, "Pre-Death Experiences: A Hospice Physician's Perspective on Spirituality and the Terminally Ill."

He is a frequent guest of local, national, and international media. Dr. Lerma is creating a non-profit company titled Hearts without Borders, which will take the hospice concept to underserved areas in South America. His organization's current project is to organize a hospice team and travel to several Mexican and South American cities to aid governments and physicians in giving birth to the wonderful gift of hospice.